UNDERSTANDING
GARY SHTEYNGART

UNDERSTANDING CONTEMPORARY AMERICAN LITERATURE

Matthew J. Bruccoli, Founding Editor

Linda Wagner-Martin, Series Editor

UNDERSTANDING
GARY SHTEYNGART

Geoff Hamilton

The University of South Carolina Press

Published by the University of South Carolina Press
Columbia, South Carolina 29208

www.sc.edu/uscpress

Manufactured in the United States of America

26 25 24 23 22 21 20 19 18 17 10 9 8 7 6 5 4 3 2 1

Library of Congress Cataloging-in-Publication Data
can be found at http://catalog.loc.gov/.

ISBN: 978-1-61117-764-0 (hardcover)
ISBN: 978-1-61117-765-7 (ebook)

This book was printed on recycled paper with 30 percent
postconsumer waste content.

For Sharlyn

CONTENTS

Series Editor's Preface ix

Acknowledgments xi

Chapter 1
Understanding Gary Shteyngart 1

Chapter 2
The Russian Debutante's Handbook 17

Chapter 3
Absurdistan 37

Chapter 4
Super Sad True Love Story 57

Chapter 5
Little Failure 77

Chapter 6
Gary Shteyngart and American Literary Celebrity 95

Notes 111

Bibliography 131

Index 139

SERIES EDITOR'S PREFACE

The Understanding Contemporary American Literature series was founded by the estimable Matthew J. Bruccoli (1931–2008), who envisioned these volumes as guides or companions for students as well as good nonacademic readers, a legacy that will continue as new volumes are developed to fill in gaps among the nearly one hundred series volumes published to date and to embrace a host of new writers only now making their marks on our literature.

As Professor Bruccoli explained in his preface to the volumes he edited, because much influential contemporary literature makes special demands, "the word understanding in the titles was chosen deliberately. Many willing readers lack an adequate understanding of how contemporary literature works; that is, of what the author is attempting to express and the means by which it is conveyed." Aimed at fostering this understanding of good literature and good writers, the criticism and analysis in the series provide instruction in how to read certain contemporary writers—explicating their material, language, structures, themes, and perspectives—and facilitate a more profitable experience of the works under discussion.

In the twenty-first century Professor Bruccoli's prescience gives us an avenue to publish expert critiques of significant contemporary American writing. The series continues to map the literary landscape and to provide both instruction and enjoyment. Future volumes will seek to introduce new voices alongside canonized favorites, to chronicle the changing literature of our times, and to remain, as Professor Bruccoli conceived, contemporary in the best sense of the word.

Linda Wagner-Martin, Series Editor

ACKNOWLEDGMENTS

Many thanks go to Tony Fong, Brian Jones, Simon Rogers, Anton Titov, and Tom Venetis for their invaluable help in reading and strengthening drafts of this book.

CHAPTER 1

Understanding Gary Shteyngart

Few contemporary authors have met with the combination of critical and commercial success enjoyed by Gary Shteyngart. He arrived as a literary star in 2002 with *The Russian Debutante's Handbook*—a novel largely responsible for propelling an enduring surge of Russian American writing—and confirmed his place on the American literary scene with two more novels, *Absurdistan* (2006) and *Super Sad True Love Story* (2010), and a memoir, *Little Failure* (2014), each of which has garnered prestigious prizes and become a national bestseller. Shteyngart's oeuvre also includes acclaimed travel writing for the *New York Times,* the *New Yorker,* and *Travel + Leisure;* YouTube videos featuring Hollywood stars such as James Franco and Paul Giamatti; and a stunning number of blurbs for others' works (endorsements that are themselves the source of a cult following on Tumblr and a documentary by the author and television writer Jonathan Ames). No longer just a literary name, Shteyngart is by now well established as a literary personality, and he engages much of his current readership (and future readers) online, as a celebrity known for his comic persona: a not-quite-assimilated Russian Jewish immigrant, amusingly dishevelled and blundering, part Slavic clown, part schlemiel.

One obvious attraction of Shteyngart as an author is his brilliance as a comic writer. Michiko Kakutani, reviewing *Little Failure* in the *New York Times,* has put it well: "Of the many enormously gifted authors now writing about the immigrant experience—including Jhumpa Lahiri, Edwidge Danticat, Dinaw Mengestu, Chang-rae Lee, Chimamanda Ngozi Adichie and Gish Jen—Gary Shteyngart is undoubtedly the funniest (with Junot Díaz a close runner-up)."[1] Shteyngart's voice has evolved since his literary debut—a manic, sprawling farce that the author himself now seems interested in disavowing[2]—but all his work is distinguished by a delightful exuberance and ingenuity, a playfulness that often moves arrestingly into the grotesque.

Shteyngart is also an exceptionally astute observer and satirist of contemporary life. He has deftly explored the intricacies of identity politics in the twenty-first century, and his manipulation of multiple literary traditions has revised seminal mythologies of racial and ethnic belonging in cannily playful ways. Often characterized as a "Russian American" author (and, less commonly, a Jewish American one), he has particularly illuminated the exilic conditions of Russian Jewish identities in the United States, as well as across the global diaspora of Russians and Jews. With the publication of *Super Sad True Love Story,* which presents a near-future American dystopia, Shteyngart has broadened his thematic foci by engaging some of the most profound and rapidly developing social transformations of the modern era. The novel—his most ambitious and significant work thus far—provides insights into the (sur) reality of hyper-technologized, globally-networked life, and vivid depictions of the impact of social networking culture on privacy, civility, literacy, sexual expression, and material consumption. Though he has sometimes been dismissed as simply an "immigrant author" performing a rather marginal ethnic shtick, Shteyngart's work deserves analysis for its remarkable centrality: its relevance to core questions of identity-formation and belonging, and of tradition and the conditions of belief, common to globalized societies.

Shteyngart, an only child, was born Igor Semyonovich Shteyngart in 1972, in what was then Leningrad in the Soviet Union. His parents were relatively prosperous: his mother taught piano at a kindergarten, and his father pursued a "generally uninspiring career engineering large telescopes at the famous LOMO photography factory."[3] They apparently were not well matched—his father's village origins clashed with his mother's big-city background—and much of their relationship seems to have been acrimonious. Shteyngart recalls his Russian childhood as being marked by both emotional and physical stresses: he suffered from severe asthma and had to endure his parents' painful and ineffectual folk remedies. This affliction perhaps contributed to a lifelong sense of spiritual suffocation, linked for him with familial discord and personal suffering. As he described one particularly traumatic episode in his memoir: "My breathing goes shallow. . . . I take off my pajamas and dutifully lie down on my stomach. My parents, still screaming at each other in two languages [Russian and Yiddish], prepare the cupping kit, getting the rubbing alcohol ready to feed the flames. A mere decade later I will find a new space to fill with alcohol."[4]

In 1978 the Shteyngarts took advantage of an opportunity to leave their homeland, joining a large and growing Jewish emigration from the Soviet Union, made possible by a deal struck between President Carter and General Secretary Brezhnev (by the end of the twentieth century, approximately six hundred thousand Soviet Jews had arrived in North America).[5] After stopping for several months in Austria and Italy as they worked out their passage west, the family finally settled in Queens, New York, beginning life as impoverished and deracinated—but optimistic and energetic—Americans. Shteyngart's father sought to deepen the family's religious identity in the United States, and so he enrolled his son in the Solomon Schechter School, an institution devoted to conservative Judaism. Shteyngart knew as little Hebrew as he did English, however, and his experience at the school thus compounded his disorientation in the United States. A difficult process of acculturation followed as Shteyngart's parents struggled to find gainful employment and he puzzled out his identity as a Russian-speaking Jew, an oddly dressed, heavily accented "Stinky Russian Bear"[6] in the eyes and noses of his young classmates. A particularly harrowing episode during this period was his botched circumcision at eight years of age, an event he would fictionalize in *Absurdistan:* "the procedure at the public hospital did not go well. . . . There will be creatures in horror movies in my near future, the softshell crabs of Ridley Scott's *Alien* the most visually accomplished ones, but this baroque chiaroscuro of dried blood and thread will never find equal."[7] Shteyngart's keen sense of being an outsider, and of having to work hard to understand, and somehow meet, the expectations of his social milieu, began with this difficult assumption of a Russian Jewish American identity.

So strong was cold-war hysteria in Reagan's America, Shteyngart has recalled, that it made sense to him to assume—or attempt to assume—an ostensibly less threatening ethnicity among his young peers:

> . . . one day after one Commie comment too many, I tell my fellow pupils that I wasn't born in Russia at all. Yes, I just remembered it! It had all been a big misunderstanding! I was actually born in Berlin, right next to Flughafen Berlin-Schönefeld, surely you've heard of it.
>
> So here I am trying to convince Jewish children in Hebrew school that I am actually a German.
>
> And can't these little bastards see that I love America more than anyone loves America? I am a ten-year-old Republican. I believe that taxes should only be levied on the poor, and the rest of Americans should be left alone. But how do I bridge that gap between being Russian and being loved?[8]

A temporary and partial answer to that question, Shteyngart discovered, was to write imaginative stories, many of them incorporating elements of science fiction, a genre he would explore as an adult in *Super Sad True Love Story*. One of his first efforts, a novella called *The Chalenge,* reflected his own anxieties about stigmatized identities in its depiction of "a race war in outer space," as did a later effort featuring a villainous cabal called "The Academy of Moors."[9] Prefiguring his later satirical thrusts at conservative Judaism and religiosity more generally (a thematic preoccupation in *Absurdistan*), he composed his own version of the Torah: "[It] is a hatchet job directed at the entirety of the SSSQ [Solomon Schechter School of Queens] religious experience, the rote memorization of ancient texts, the aggressive shouting of blessings and counterblessings before and after lunch, the ornery rabbi who claims the Jews brought on the Holocaust by their overconsumption of delicious pork products. . . . Exodus becomes Sexodus. Henry Miller would have been proud. Moses is renamed Mishugana, and instead of the Burning Bush there is the Burning Television. God sends the Australians twelve plagues, the last one of which is Rabbi Sofer, SSSQ's potbellied Hebrew principal and strongman."[10] Shteyngart's novels often engage in similar strategies of ironic renaming as they revise biblical narratives and the exploits of their protagonists.

A sympathetic teacher at Hebrew school invited Shteyngart to read his work in front of the class, allowing him to claim new prestige among the other students and develop his skills as an entertainer. As he noted in his memoir of the significance of this moment: "I am moving the children away from my Russianness and toward storytelling."[11] Though it took many years for him to become comfortable in the role of celebrity satirist, this early positive experience of renown—and of the receptiveness of others to his sardonic representations of ethnicity—profoundly shaped Shteyngart's sense of authorial vocation.

The Shteyngarts spoke Russian at home and did not own a television for much of their son's childhood, thereby providing an immersion in Russian culture. They placed the family bookcase—filled with works by Pushkin, Tolstoy, Chekhov, and Dostoevsky—in his room and encouraged him to read literary classics in their native tongue. Through the 1980s the family steadily ascended to middle-class solidity. Though Shteyngart's primary intellectual passion was imaginative writing, he was enrolled as a teenager in the prestigious Stuyvesant High School for the maths and sciences. Here he escaped the claustrophobic conditions of Hebrew school in a new, multicultural environment, the students largely a mix of "young, pimply Russians, Koreans, Chinese, [and] Indians" similarly striving for upward mobility. Shteyngart did not flourish academically, however, for he discovered himself to be, relative to his classmates, "a terrible student."[12] Burdened by a new sense of alienation, he cultivated a slacker persona, confirmed by experimentation with drugs and alcohol. Adrift ideologically, he looked for guidance in the pages of William F. Buckley's conservative magazine, the *National Review,* and soon proclaimed himself—to the delight of his father—a proud Republican, defender of Israel, and fierce opponent of "welfare queens."[13] He also became a member of the National Rifle Association for a time, even though, as he noted wryly in his memoir, he was "too young to own a gun and to be able to shoot a black person on the subway who might rob me."[14]

In 1991 Shteyngart entered Ohio's Oberlin College and somewhat ambivalently committed himself to studies in politics and creative writing. The school's liberal environment, a frequent satirical target in his first two novels, helped terminate any affiliation with his father's pragmatic conservatism and widened the long-developing intellectual divide between them: "On his first visit to Oberlin my father stood on a giant vagina painted in the middle of the quad by the campus lesbian, gay, and bisexual organization, oblivious to the rising tide of hissing and camp around him, as he enumerated to me the differences between laser-jet and ink-jet printers, specifically the price points of the cartridges. If I'm not mistaken, he thought he was standing on a peach."[15]

Shteyngart was relieved to find that Oberlin's intellectual standards were far less rigorous than Stuyvesant High's, and he managed to maintain top academic standing while enthusiastically indulging in alcohol and marijuana. Immersed in a student body largely composed of wealthy students with a fondness for Marxist ideals (but little knowledge of those who had actually lived under communist regimes), Shteyngart developed a new awareness of the prestige associated with his Russian background. A significant dimension of his education at Oberlin involved learning how to negotiate, with increasing cynicism, his claim to an esteemed place among the dispossessed: "Here the great arias of self-involvement . . . wind their way through the boxy little classrooms as professors eagerly facilitate our growth as social beings and master complainers."[16] Though his attempts at Oberlin to write about the Soviet world were unsuccessful according to his own and others' judgements, his college experience helped him establish a fundamental authorial identity—a Russian exiled in America—that would ultimately inform his breakout fiction.

After graduating from Oberlin, Shteyngart returned to New York City and worked at a number of jobs, including a stint at the New York Association for New Arrivals, where he helped recent immigrants adjust to American life. He also continued to craft a novel, originally titled *The Pyramids of Prague,* begun at college. This work—a sprawling farce set largely in the Czech Republic, where he had spent a term as an exchange student—was initially rejected by elite creative writing programs to which Shteyngart had applied, but it eventually caught the attention of fellow novelist Chang-rae Lee.[17] With Lee's recommendation Shteyngart's manuscript, now called *The Russian Debutante's*

Handbook, found a home at Penguin Putnam and was published in 2002 to significant acclaim. In 2007, following the publication of his second novel, Shteyngart joined Columbia University's creative writing department. He married a Korean American woman named Esther Won in 2010, and they greeted their first child in 2013.

Shteyngart's *Little Failure* offers an amusing reflection—with characteristic pathos—on the origins of his own name: "Let's start with my surname: Shteyngart. A German name whose insane Sovietized spelling, eye-watering bunching of consonants (just one i between the h and t and you got some pretty nice 'Shit' there), and overall unattractiveness has cost me a lot of human warmth."[18] As he explained, the name itself was mangled by some mysterious administrative process during his grandfather's journey from rural Ukraine to Leningrad:

> Recently I found out from my father that Shteyngart is not our name at all. A slip of the pen in some Soviet official's hand, a drunk notary, a semiliterate commissar, who knows, but I am not really Gary Shteyngart. My family name is—Steinhorn. Meaning "Stone Horn." Though I was born Igor—my name was changed to Gary in America so that I would suffer one or two fewer beatings—my Leningrad birth certificate should have welcomed into this world one Citizen Igor Stone Horn. I have clearly spent thirty-nine years unaware that my real destiny was to go through life as a Bavarian porn star, but some further questions present themselves: If neither Gary nor Shteyngart is truly my name, then what the hell am I doing calling myself Gary Shteyngart? Is every single cell in my body a historical lie?[19]

Anxieties over the names one has been given, and those one would claim, are in fact presiding themes in Shteyngart's fiction. A sense of being the dupe of history, misnamed and misplaced among cultures, is common to his protagonists, who share an exilic sensibility and often dream of returning to some authentic and typically fantastical homeland. One's proper name and place cannot, Shteyngart's narratives insist, simply be taken for granted, and finding them involves intricate processes of negotiation between one's fantasies and the world's recalcitrant demands. The formation of selfhood in fact often becomes a matter of highly contested rhetorical struggle, with one's identity a shimmering, elusive victory to be achieved rather than a stable endowment received as a birthright. These assumptions are central to Shteyngart's first novel, *The Russian Debutante's Handbook,* in which Vladimir Girshkin, homeless wherever he goes, attempts to pass himself off to others and himself as either an American or a Russian and is reminded at last that for some he can only be a Jew. Misha Vainberg, the globe-trotting protagonist of *Absurdistan,* just as earnestly—but even less adroitly—balances Russian, American, and Jewish affiliations, while being physically barred from returning to the United States itself. *Super Sad True Love Story* gives us not just a protagonist but an entire culture involved in manic self-creation and quests to escape even the mortal limits placed on identity.

Though his brief childhood years in Leningrad were not idyllic, they seem to suggest for Shteyngart a kind of quasi-Edenic state, separate from the rupture with which the rest of his life—and his writing—began. As he remarked in a 2002 interview, "It sounds weird, but I loved my Soviet childhood. . . . The Communist life suited me just great. I loved the Red Army and everything. It only became horrible once you were an adult."[20] All Shteyngart's work in fact seems dominated by a fundamental imaginative backdrop: the decline and fall of the Soviet Union he knew in his early youth and the various transformations undergone by the post-Soviet world since his immigration to America. Shteyngart's first two novels explore the highly polarized wealth distribution, ascendance of organized crime networks, and general sense of cultural degeneration in that world, while his third examines the essential merging of Soviet-style totalitarianism with American hedonism and capitalist excess in the near future. In his memoir *Little Failure,* Shteyngart returns to St. Petersburg (formerly Leningrad) with his parents in order to comprehend his family's origins and the Soviet-era traumas they have not been able to leave behind. The deadening spiritual effects of late capitalism are a thematic preoccupation for many contemporary American writers, but, unlike many of his peers, Shteyngart combines his critique of the West's consumer culture with a wistful respect for at least some aspects of communism. As Nataša Kovačević argued of *The Russian Debutante's Handbook,* "Shteyngart views the grand narrative of communism, or at least belief in it, with a dose of nostalgia, contrasting the collectivist idealism of Eastern European communists with the disaffected, cynical crowds inhabiting post-communist societies, thriving on spectacular consumption that stretches from East to West."[21] Though the intensity and earnestness of this nostalgia wane from his second novel onward, a yearning for some kind of "collectivist idealism"—a source of belonging that exceeds the isolating comforts of Western individualism—runs through all Shteyngart's work.

One also discovers here a strong suggestion that what was best about his homeland has been ruined in part by exposure to global capitalism. Shteyngart's explorations of the post-Soviet world often underscore the corrosive influence of the West on the cultural integrity of the East: glamorous images of Western lifestyles inspire a vulgar mimicry in Eastern consumers, supplanting distinctive local cultures with homogenized, placeless ones. The American expatriates in *The Russian Debutante's Handbook* have, in the eyes of that novel's protagonist, largely corrupted the traditional charms of "Prava" (a stand-in for Prague)[22] as they drive the historical city's transition to a modern consumer paradise. In *Absurdistan*—set in a nation strongly resembling Azerbaijan—the forces of globalization have given even a desperately poor nation a startling capitalist makeover:

> We taxied past a billboard. Three stylish teenagers, a redheaded beauty, an Asian beauty, and a young black man in dreadlocks (a feminine beauty in his own right), critically regarded us with their handsome, expressionless eyes. THE UNITED COLORS OF BENETTON WELCOME YOU TO SVANÏ CITY, the billboard read.
>
> In keeping with the progressive theme, the arrivals terminal was newly built to resemble a post-Mongolian yurt made of tinted glass, corrugated steel, and the occasional exposed pipe—the kind of generic design favored by mineral-rich nations teetering between Eastern exotica and Western anonymity. Inside, we found a cool, open metallic shed layered with the smells of perfume counters and stores dispensing freshly baked baguettes along with the most cultured of yogurts, the small flags of the world's countries and the oversize flag of Microsoft Windows NT limply hanging from the rafters to remind us that we were all global citizens who loved to travel and compute.[23]

Shteyngart's own American acculturation rapidly increased—and his immersion in Russian culture declined—after his parents gave in and bought a television, allowing him to consume a pop-culture cornucopia that displaced Chekhov and Dostoevsky with *The Brady Bunch, Gilligan's Island, Three's Company,* and *The Six-Million-Dollar Man.* In the Soviet Union of his youth, he comically noted in his memoir, television had relatively little to offer and was actually physically dangerous: "The television is an object of great consternation among Soviet citizens because it regularly explodes. At one point, 60 percent of the house fires in Moscow are said to be caused by poorly assembled exploding television sets."[24] As the sociologist Anthony Giddens explained, the collapse of the Soviet Union had much to do with the impact of mass media:

> Globalization explains both why and how Soviet communism met its end. The former Soviet Union and the East European countries were comparable to the West in terms of growth rates until somewhere around the early 1970s. After that point, they fell rapidly behind. Soviet communism, with its emphasis upon state-run enterprise and heavy industry, could not compete in the global electronic economy. The ideological and cultural control upon which communist political authority was based similarly could not survive in an era of global media. . . . The Soviet and the East European regimes

> were unable to prevent the reception of Western radio and television broadcasts. Television played a direct role in the 1989 revolutions, which have rightly been called the first 'television revolutions.[25]

In his first two novels, Shteyngart charted—through the distorting lens of wild satire—the range of upheavals produced by those revolutions and the eventual collapse of the Soviet Union. Throughout the 1990s, living standards declined, unemployment rose, and wealth was polarized in Russia and the former Soviet republics, producing a large impoverished class and a small group of extremely powerful oligarchs. Among the blights afflicting the post-Soviet world were the criminal networks that rose in power and sophistication after the collapse of communism. Mafiosi are a locus of attention in *The Russian Debutante's Handbook* and *Absurdistan,* and Shteyngart's caricatures of them play on actual historical realities that had become well known by the late twentieth and early twenty-first century. As Robert I. Friedman wrote in *Red Mafiya: How the Russian Mob Has Invaded America,* these organizations have achieved over the past several decades an international reach and forbidding reputation:

> Blending financial sophistication with bone-crushing violence, the Russian mob has become the FBI's most formidable criminal adversary, creating an international criminal colossus that has surpassed the Colombian cartels, the Japanese Yakuzas, the Chinese triads, and the Italian Mafia in wealth and weaponry. . . . With activities in countries ranging from Malaysia to Great Britain, Russian mobsters now operate in more than fifty nations. They smuggle heroin from Southeast Asia, traffic in weapons all over the globe, and seem to have a special knack for large-scale extortion. . . . Tutored in the mercenary ways of a brutal totalitarian state riddled with corruption, the Russians have developed a business acumen that puts them in a class by themselves.[26]

Shteyngart's fiction seems acutely conscious, however, of the ways in which Easterners—and Russians in particular—have been depicted in Western mass media, and his fiction often toys with notions of Eastern identities (the babushka, the newly rich oligarch, the apparatchik, and others) that have become mass-media clichés. The figure of the Russian mobster is especially important to his first two novels, which traffic in caricatures of post-Soviet states that both indulge in, and subtly critique, stereotypes of Eastern criminality. A representative moment occurs in *The Russian Debutante's Handbook:* arriving at the Prava airport, Vladimir Girshkin mingles momentarily with a group of bland Westerners before being greeted by a riotous cavalcade of Mafiosi:

> . . . instantaneously as a plane falling out of the sky, the scene was russified. Small-arms fire exploded outside.
>
> A dozen car alarms engaged.
>
> A detachment of men, each with a small Kalashnikov at hip level, swiftly parted the Americans into two screaming herds.
>
> The requisite carpet was rolled out between them.
>
> A convoy of BMWs and armor-plated Range Rovers was assembled in protective formation. . . .
>
> Flanked by three associates, all aglow in their nylon sports jackets and matching space-age trousers made out of alpaca or maybe silicon, the [mobster] solemnly approached. He was a burly, pocked little man with his eyes slightly crossed and his hair parted to make the least of a disappearing hairline.[27]

The narrative implies that the reader has plunged deep into fantasy here as Russian mobsters fulfill—and in fact exceed—their cartoonish representations in a host of Western popular entertainments. In the period just before the novel was published, these range from the films *Little Odessa, The Jackal, Rounders,* and *Training Day;* to television programs such as *The Sopranos* and *Law & Order,* to the video game *Grand Theft Auto 2*. In *Absurdistan* the protagonist's father, Boris Vainberg, colorfully hyperbolizes stereotypes of the enterprising Jewish Russian racketeer: "Placed in this [prison, after being arrested for Zionist activities], Papa fronted the gangster talk. He devised all kinds of cigarette-related prison capers. He turned bread crumbs into shoe polish and shoe polish into wine. He smuggled in copies of *Penthouse,* pasted the centrefolds on the back of a willing inmate with girlish hips and rented him out by the hour. By the time Beloved Papa got out, two things had happened: Gorbachev had graciously called off most of that annoying, unprofitable communism with the long lines and detonating television sets, and Beloved Papa had met everyone he would need to know in his reincarnation as a Russian oligarch."[28] Vainberg seems to have been named after an actual Russian Jewish gangster named Ludwig "Tarzan" Fainberg, who became a celebrity after a series of journalistic profiles and television documentaries recounted his misdeeds and whose most infamous caper involved negotiating the sale of a former Soviet submarine to Colombian drug dealers.[29]

It is not just Shteyngart's fiction but also the authorial persona he has cultivated in interviews and through marketing campaigns that has encouraged audiences to identify him as a spokesman for all things "Russian," with an insider's knowledge of the seedier elements of post-Soviet life. Shortly after the publication of *The Russian Debutante's Handbook* in 2002, a lengthy author profile of Shteyngart titled "From Russia with Tsoris"—"tsoris" being Yiddish for "trouble and suffering"—appeared in the *New York Times*. Shteyngart was presented here—and presented, as it were, presenting himself—as a kind of native Russian informant, a rare source of sensational Eastern esoterica.

> Draining his third glass of horseradish vodka [at the Russian Samovar restaurant], Gary Shteyngart is starting to feel chummy. Sliding over on the curved banquette, the young novelist asks to show me some photographs—snapshots, he says, of a recent trip he took in the "disaster of my homeland, the former Soviet Union."
>
> Shteyngart hands over the first picture: a poorly composed shot of a nondescript urban plaza. "Oh, this is a great one!" he says. "This is Tbilisi, Georgia. One night, I was chased down this street right here by a man with a knife!" He smiles wistfully. "The guy had just lost it somehow; he was crazy with despair. You see it all the time there. I went back the next day to memorialize the event."
>
> He flips to a photo of several hirsute men sitting around a banquet table. Shteyngart, who is in this picture, fits right in: his jet-black goatee is so dense and bristly that you could shine your shoes with it. "I spent a long weekend outside Tbilisi," he explains, "with some guys who were trying to . . . recruit me." In the snapshot, a grinning Shteyngart is holding up an enormous ram's horn. "It was a ceremonial toast," he says. "They were excited, I think, because they thought they'd succeeded in getting a clever Jew from New York to help them with a scheme." The plot, he adds cryptically, "had to do with American charities." (He declined to participate.) So are these acquaintances mafiya? "Let me put it this way," he says wryly. "This 24-year-old here is practically the only guy in the country with a Porsche."[30]

There is clearly some ironic mischievousness in this pitch of insider "authenticity" and special knowing—if less pronounced than in Shteyngart's actual fiction—that seems to acknowledge the rising popularity of the "Russian brand" in the American literary marketplace. Alexandra Tatarsky noted the twenty-first century "vogue for Russian American immigrant fiction [that] has turned into a fully fledged literary boom"—her inventory included writing by Ellen Litman, David Bezmozgis, Alina Simone, Lara Vapnyar, Anya Ulinich, Yelena Akhtiorskaya, Kseniya Melnik, and Boris Fishman—and suggested that much of this work seems deliberately crafted as caricature, at least in part: "The books share this tendency towards meta-narrative in which the protagonist functions as something of an alter-ego for the author, musing on Russianness, on writing and on writing about Russianness—with a self-consciousness that verges on self-parody. This exaggeration of Russianness allows the writer to capitalise on the current marketability of Russian-American literature while also making fun of it."[31] A curious irony of Shteyngart's self-constructions as a Russian, which become increasingly self-conscious in *Absurdistan* and in his author interviews after the publication of that novel, is that he has seemingly had to play, and play up, the role of Russian to Americans in order to become a successful author, whereas as a child he had to act the role of an American, leaving behind obvious markers of his Russianness in order to be accepted by his young peers.

Reviews of Shteyngart's work often invoke a series of Russian precursors with whom he is said to share an essential affinity. Nikolai Gogol is the author most often cited, presumably because of the similarity between the authors' dark and outrageous satirical mode. In a 2014 interview Shteyngart remarked on the centrality of that mode to Russian literature, citing Gogol as exemplary of the national tradition with which he links himself: "It's a very Russian thing, a very Soviet thing. The greatest books in Russian literature are satires. Gogol's *Dead Souls,* for example, is a very over-the-top satire about life in Russia. I think it's the thing we do best."[32] Both Gogol's "divided" ethnicity and his relationship to the material of his novel intriguingly parallel Shteyngart's, for as a native Ukrainian, Gogol's "Russian" credentials were suspect to some, and he did not have much first-hand knowledge of the region he explored at a significant geographical distance. In response to a query about his own ethnicity, Gogol affirmed his own "blended" status:

> I'll tell you that I myself don't know what soul I have: Ukrainian [*khokhlatskaia*] or Russian. I only know that I would grant primacy neither to a Little Russian over a Russian nor to a Russian over a Little Russian. Both natures are generously endowed by God, and as if on purpose, each of them in its own way includes in itself that which the other lacks—a clear sign that they are meant to complement each other. Moreover, the very stories of their past way of life are dissimilar, so that the different strengths of their characters could develop and, having then united, could become something more perfect in humanity.[33]

Shteyngart's Jewish identity further complicates his ethnic positioning, since his family, as Soviet Jews, were considered cultural outsiders in Russia. And since Soviet Jews were typically not devout—given the state's aggressive suppression of Jewish religious practices—when they immigrated to other countries, they were often not assumed to be "authentic" Jews by the Jewish population in their adopted homelands, a judgment that Shteyngart's early experiences at the Solomon Schechter School confirmed. As Adrian Wanner explained in his pioneering study *Out of Russia: Fictions of a New Translingual Diaspora,*

Paradoxically, these Soviet Jews only became "Russians" after they left Russia. Their provenance from the Soviet Union (which, in the popular conception of their host societies, was often conflated with "Russia") and their Russian native language automatically conferred on them a Russian identity in the eyes of their new compatriots. At the same time, their status as Jews, which had allowed them to emigrate in the first place, came under question in light of their secularity and ignorance of the Jewish faith and Jewish tradition. As a result, they were seen as not Jewish "enough," or even as not Jewish at all, by their fellow Jews in their host countries.[34]

Soviet Jews settling in their new homes often felt, understandably, a profound sense of compounded cultural estrangement. Categorizing their diasporic affiliation, as Olga Gershenson and David Schneer have pointed out, also poses a number of conceptual challenges: "Post-Soviet Jews, who often maintain multiple passports, multiple homes, and multiple languages, make us rethink the meaning of homeland and exile: are they part of a traditional Jewish diaspora or a new Russian diaspora? Transnational post-Soviet Jews are rapidly becoming one of the newest and most important subjects of study as Jewish studies become more global."[35]

In the twenty-first century, as Gershenson and Schneer note, "post-Soviet Jewry is transforming American Jewish literature."[36] Shteyngart's work has made seminal contributions to that transformation, for it directly engages and astutely explores the complex questions of belonging generated by the global Jewish diaspora. Moreover, the broad commercial success of his works—which far exceeds that of peers such as Lara Vapnyar, Ellen Litman, Anya Ulinich, or David Bezmozgis—has raised these evolving definitions of Jewish identity to a remarkable prominence within American literary culture. Though close analysis should add nuance to Gershenson and Schneer's observation that Shteyngart's novels "feature essentially the same protagonist—an American-raised Russian Jewish son to émigré parents, forever torn between languages, cultures, and heritages,"[37] these works (along with Shteyngart's memoir, *Little Failure*) indeed reveal the complex, emerging negotiations involved in Russian Jewish American identities.[38]

Shteyngart's negotiations of his own identity have sometimes been challenged by academic critics. A recurring criticism of his first novel—which he satirically addresses in his second—is that its claims to "Russianness" are somehow counterfeit, part of a strained attempt to appropriate a culture that is not quite the author's own. Mikhail Iossel, delivering a mock address to a group of Russian American authors meant to include Shteyngart, put the point colorfully:

> Dear hypothetical Soviet émigré children out there! God love you, but let me just resolve your doubts on this account: you are Americans, at least the great majority of you; American English is your native language . . . and you are Americans, which is wonderful, all irony aside, just the bees knees, and I am a U.S. citizen, but you have no more direct connection to Russia than I do to the NBA: you have connection to the Soviet-Jewish or Russian émigré community in the U.S., and it is just not the same. So it's ok to stop wringing your figurative hands and feeling oh so blue about how torn you are with regards to your identity. Nabokov never wrote about his inner torment and being torn, about the ferocious struggle taking place within his being concerning his true identity. Neither did Brodsky. . . . Because they were grownups and knew who they were and knew, too, that talking about your inner torment (especially a somewhat artificial, manufactured one) is a little, well, unseemly.[39]

Adrian Wanner noted that Russian critics have tended to ignore or disparage Shteyngart's oeuvre, along with other Russian American writing, and he pointed out the peculiarity of Shteyngart's strong claim to a Russian identity, given that he left the former Soviet Union as a young child and seems to have little positive to say about his former home. Wanner conceded, however, that "there can be no doubt that Shteyngart's identification with Russian culture is genuine."[40]

Shteyngart's embrace by American Jews would seem to be confirmed by his winning the National Jewish Book Award and the Goldberg Prize for Emerging Writers of Jewish Fiction for *The Russian Debutante's Handbook;* he has been lauded by at least one prominent Jewish American critic, Donald Weber, as representing, along with Lara Vapnyar and David Bezmozgis, "a fascinating new chapter in a long tradition of Jewish immigrant writing."[41] Others have raised concerns, however, about Shteyngart's trafficking in stereotypes and supposed distortion of the values and experiences of other post-Soviet Jews. Marat Grinberg, for instance, has accused Shteyngart of "hollowing out" Soviet Jewishness and unfairly proffering his own family's interpersonal dysfunction, ignorance of Judaism and festering racism as broadly representative.[42] Adam Rovner offered a subtler critique of Shteyngart's and Bezmozgis's portrayals of Jews in his influential article "So Easily Assimilated: The *New* Immigrant Chic." Assimilated American Jews may feel haunted by a sense that they are not quite distinct *enough* in the nation's twenty-first century cultural mosaic, argued Rovner, and authors such as Shteyngart and Bezmozgis have offered a compelling but spurious confirmation of Jewish separateness and ostensible authenticity: "What I am suggesting is that the sometimes frantic American

Jewish search for roots derives from our sense—right or wrong—of having been so easily assimilated during the last hundred or so years since Jewish immigration peaked in 1907. Quite simply, our loss of manifest difference—religious, ethnic, linguistic, and geographic—has entailed a concomitant desire to assert some difference in our cultural artifacts."[43] Shteyngart's presumed exotic alterity remains, in other words, a matter of fantasy projection.

One of the American authors with whom Shteyngart is often compared is Philip Roth, who similarly rose to literary stardom in his twenties with highly autobiographical fiction (winning the National Book Award in 1959 for *Goodbye, Columbus*), and courted controversy among Jewish readers with his comically unflattering representations of Jews. His novel *Portnoy's Complaint* (1969) seems particularly aligned with Shteyngart's work in terms of its indifference to ethnic pieties, frank exploration of sexual taboos, and astonishing linguistic verve. As Joe Moran remarked, in a description that could easily fit Shteyngart, Roth made a conscious turn with this novel to combine "European literary influences (Chekhov, Tolstoy, Flaubert, Mann and Kafka)" with "a freer verbal facility suggestive of oral performance, influenced by the comedy routines of Abbott and Costello and the Marx Brothers and several years of psychoanalysis."[44] Shteyngart's writing—which also owes something to the verbal antics of Joseph Heller's *Catch-22*—is particularly lively in its rendering of dialogue. This dimension of his work, as he explained in a recent interview, is especially important to his ambitions as an artist:

> The operative word I think really is "act." There's a reason I'm doing these [YouTube book] trailers: I love to act, I've always wanted to be an actor. I think that acting and fiction go nicely together—being able to visualize language as something you perform, not just something that's there on the page. That's why it was so great to have James Franco in my writing class [at Columbia University]. A big problem with fiction is that you read dialogue, and it's dialogue that writers think has to be dialogue because it's the way it's been over the centuries. There's nothing alive about it. I look for stuff that sings off the page when I write, whether it's a memoir or one of my novels. I act out the whole thing. I listen to the dialogue, I try to recreate what it would sound like. If it sounds false, if the bullshit meter goes off, I can't include it.[45]

Shteyngart has an especially gifted ear for the rhythms of idiomatic English. *Absurdistan* adroitly and comically ventriloquizes, for instance, Russian mobsters, African American hip hop artists, working-class Puerto Rican Americans, idealistic multiculturalists, Park Avenue psychotherapists, and native English speakers *attempting* to sound like clumsy second-language speakers. The high point of Shteyngart's virtuoso impressions comes in *Super Sad True Love Story,* in which he transforms the crudeness of contemporary linguistic degradation—the illiteracy and inarticulateness of a youth-obsessed culture—into uproarious, and often poignant, comedy.

And like Philip Roth—who became infamous for the vivid sexual content of *Portnoy's Complain,* and augmented his reputation as a chronicler of explicit sexual confessions with *Sabbath's Theater* (1995)—Shteyngart has become known for a particularly outrageous kind of erotic subject matter. *The Russian Debutante's Handbook* includes vivid passages concerning the perverse sex lives of gangsters, while *Absurdistan* goes much further in exploring inventive and bizarre permutations of bedroom slapstick. Though *Super Sad True Love Story* includes copious explicit material too, Shteyngart departs here from a predominantly farcical tone and evokes more gently both the comedy and pathos of human sexuality:

> With my mind's eye floating over my bald spot and, beneath that, the thick tendrils of Eunice's mane spilling over three supportive pillows, I saw her strong, vital legs with their half-moon calves and between them the chalky white bulk of me moored, righted, held in place for life. I saw the tanned, boyish body beneath me, and the new summertime freckles, and the alert nipples that formed tight brown capsules between my fingers, and felt the melody of her garlicky, sweet, slightly turned breath—and I began, with the kind of insistence that brings out heart attacks in men six years older than myself, to plunge in and out of Eunice's tightness, a desperate animal growl filtering out of my lungs. Eunice's eyes, wet and compassionate, watched me do what I needed to do. Unlike others of her generation, she was not completely steeped in pornography, and so the instinct for sex came from somewhere else inside her; it spoke of the need for warmth instead of debasement. She lifted up her head, enveloping me with her own heat, and bit the soft protuberance of my lower lip. "Don't leave me, Lenny," she whispered into my ear. "Don't please ever leave me."[46]

The unironic earnestness of this plea—its grounding in a world of genuine suffering, no matter the ludicrous atmosphere in which it takes place—more broadly suggests the direction in which Shteyngart's writing has moved since the publication of his first novel.

CHAPTER 2

The Russian Debutante's Handbook

Shteyngart's first novel—nearly five hundred pages in length—introduces us to Vladimir Girshkin, a Russian Jewish émigré to New York who is roughly the same age as the author, with a domineering mother (she half-kiddingly calls him "*Failurchka,*" Little Failure[1]) and an undergraduate degree from a prestigious midwestern liberal arts college. With his satiric doppelganger, Shteyngart explores not just an outlandish version of his own history of assimilation and cultural nostalgia, but the general conditions of hybridized identity that have become common in contemporary American life.[2]

Vladimir is, the narrator tells us, a mercurial blend of American and Russian myth, "part P. T. Barnum, part V. I. Lenin."[3] The novel opens with him working unhappily as a junior clerk at the Emma Lazarus Immigrant Absorption Society, doing his part to help "assimilate the masses."[4] A disappointment to his parents—who hope he will follow them in aspiring to upper-middle-class solidity—Vladimir turns twenty-five without a clear sense of personal ambition. Unhappy in love, he exchanges his Jewish girlfriend Challah (Hebrew: "a special holiday bread") for a wealthy gentile named Francesca (Italian *franco:* "the free one"), but feels alienated by her condescension toward him as a first-generation immigrant and Jew. His life changes dramatically, however, after meeting one Aleksander Rybakov (Russian *rybak*: "fisherman"), a Russian exile and self-proclaimed psychotic who promises him a lucrative job in Eastern Europe in return for help securing American citizenship. After a series of misadventures that confirms his sense of estrangement from fellow Americans, Vladimir accepts Rybakov's offer and relocates to the fictional city of Prava (Russian: "right" or "correct").[5] The city is located in the equally fictional

Republic of Stolovaya (Russian: "canteen"). He partners there with Rybakov's son, a gangster nicknamed the Groundhog, first specializing in a Ponzi scheme targeting young Western expatriates, then branching out into the distribution of narcotics. The collapse of his criminal career prompts his return home—not to immigrant-rich New York, but to Cleveland, a midwestern sanctuary of stolid Americana where he marries and goes to work in middle management for his father-in-law.

Western reviews have often mentioned the novel's affiliation with Russian literature, along with its exploration of conventional American themes, including the immigrant's negotiation of a New World self. A starred Kirkus review called the work "Ambitious, funny, intelligent, in love with irony and literary allusions, as if by a lighter Nabokov."[6] Writing in *New York Magazine,* Daniel Mendelsohn pointed to Mikhail Bulgakov as a key influence, while characterizing the novel's protagonist as undergoing an "epic search for that most American of dreams—a meaningful identity" and suffering "from the bittersweet and unresolvable tragedy of being hyphenated—of being perennially 'neither here nor there.'"[7] A. O. Scott's *New York Times* review invoked Gogol, Bulgakov, and Vasily Aksyonov as important precursors and lauded the novel's engagement with "the classic immigrant's identity crisis,"[8] before hesitating a little over the hybridized result: "The bitter hilarity of full-scale Gogolian dementia is thwarted by a very American impulse to be nice to the characters, and to encourage them in a pursuit of happiness that hard-core Slavophiles would no doubt regard as disgustingly shallow."[9] Scott seems to have had in mind here Mikhail Bakhtin's praise for Gogol as a satirist who "is not light-hearted" but "sullen and gloomy to the extreme."[10]

Several reviewers have grouped Shteyngart with other novelists exploring the adventures of young American men in postcommunist Eastern Europe. Taylor Antrim's *New York Times* review linked *The Russian Debutante's Handbook* with Arthur Phillips's *Prague* and John Beckman's *Winter Zoo,* which were said to share "the same basic plot: young man graduates from college circa 1990, undergoes crisis and rushes into the warm embrace of Eastern Europe."[11] Eliot Borenstein, in his assessment of six similarly themed novels in the *Nation,* added Jonathan Franzen's *The Corrections,* Jonathan Safran Foer's *Everything Is Illuminated,* and Paul Greenberg's *Leaving Katya* to the list of contemporary American novels covering territory similar to Shteyngart's. Common to these works, Borenstein argued, is a "fundamentally male narrative of conquest, submission and coming-of-age."[12]

In the years since the novel's publication, several critics have offered incisive appraisals of its presiding themes. Natalie Friedman's "Nostalgia, Nationhood, and the New Immigrant Narrative: Gary Shteyngart's *The Russian Debutante's*

Handbook and the Post-Soviet Experience" considered Shteyngart in relation to Lara Vapnyar and David Bezmozgis, members of a "vanguard of young post-Soviet authors who immigrated to America[13] over the past thirty years and are now documenting their experiences of dislocation and deracination as they navigate not two but three cultures: the Soviet Union of their youth, their adopted nation of America, and the new post-perestroika Republics that have replaced the former Soviet Union."[14] These narratives, Friedman has argued, "destabilize the notion of Americanization and revise the idea of a genre of assimilation narratives within the subset of American ethnic writing."[15] Adam Rovner's "So Easily Assimilated: The *New* Immigrant Chic" takes up the same trio identified by Friedman—Shteyngart, Vapnyar, and Bezmozgis—in an exploration of the recent popularity of literature investigating Russian Jewish identity in contemporary North America. Common to such works, contended Rovner, is their suggestion that "Jews are *not* so easily assimilated—that they are essentially vulnerable, scared, or in some way physically marked out as Other."[16] Nataša Kovačević's chapter on Shteyngart and the Russian author Victor Pelevin in *Narrating Post/Communism: Colonial Discourse and Europe's Borderline Civilization* analyzes the novel's ambiguous critique of Western neocolonialism in its representation of an absurdly barbaric criminal class: "These figures importantly reject the position of Eastern European victims waiting to be emancipated into a global, multicultural brotherhood by Western capital, although the narrative perspective changes toward the end [of the novel], casting the mafia as Orientalized proofs of Eastern European inability to overcome its criminal nature."[17]

Among the multiple prizes claimed by *The Russian Debutante's Handbook* were the Stephen Crane Award for First Fiction and the National Jewish Book Award for Fiction. The novel did not, however, fare well in Russia. Adrian Wanner noted that its reception there was "lukewarm at best," with reviewers typically complaining that the author simply reinforced "American prejudices against Russians,"[18] masquerading as a Russian instead of presenting himself as what he clearly is in their estimation: a Jewish American. Wanner translated a review by Mikhail Vizel', from *TimeOut Moskva,* as follows: "[Shteyngart's] style and his jokes are sometimes strange and sometimes very accurate and witty, but they are always completely American. He does not have a Russian keyboard at home. This is a kind of 'immigrant novel' we have never seen before."[19]

A number of intriguing associations seem to play about the name of Shteyngart's protagonist, and it is rewarding to consider their equivocal potential as a means of framing the novel's themes. "Vladimir" carries a range of meanings in Russian that includes "power," "royalty," "peace," and "the world," and the name can be literally translated as "great global leader." Two actual Russian leaders who share the name—Vladimir Ilyich Lenin, the first premier of the Soviet state, and Vladimir Vladimirovich Putin, who had been president for about a half decade at the time of the novel's publication—may also be called to mind here; Shteyngart's Vladimir describes himself as being "born with such a big forehead that the director of the maternity ward personally congratulated his mother on giving birth to the next Vladimir Ilyich."[20] These grand connotations are ironized, however, by Vladimir's last name. The English *girsh,* rooted in an Arabic word for "coin," signifies a small monetary unit (the Russian *grosh* and the Hebrew *gerush* also mean "coin"), with the diminutive *-kin* further emphasizing a sense of triviality. The Russian word *garshok*—"a common pot," but also "a child's potty"—furnishes other suggestive shades.

And yet a deeper association seems to beckon here. There is an intriguing resemblance between the definitive first syllable of "Girshkin" and the Hebrew verb *garash,* whose core sense is "to drive, to thrust" and whose related senses include "to expel," "to plunder, to spoil," "to put forth fruit," and, in passive form, "to be expelled," "to be carried off," or "to be driven, agitated." The word first appears in the Torah in relation to the human exit from paradise: "So he drove out [*garash*] the man; and he placed at the east of the garden of Eden Cherubims, and a flaming sword which turned every way, to keep the way of the tree of life" (Genesis 3:24). Agitated by a sense of unbelonging and seduced by a compensatory fantasy of "global rule," Vladimir seeks, as it were, to thrust himself into a more fitting role, one in which he can expel the vacillating aspects of his personality and plunder the riches of a new home. He temporarily bears the fruits of a powerful new identity before being violently driven away.[21]

Consider also the distinctiveness of Vladimir's particular kind of exile. Though there is something involuntary about his movements—as a child he departs the Soviet Union with his parents, relocates to Prava partly in order to evade a gangster he has offended, and finally returns to the United States so that he might escape another group of gangsters—he is above all an exile in *sensibility,* allied with and yet barred from two homelands, who chooses to move between them in order to negotiate a satisfactory sense of belonging. His experiences may be conveyed satirically and be steeped in ironies that can seem to destabilize any fixed significance, but they ultimately speak cogently to a condition of self-exile common to contemporary America—and indeed, given the seminal and enduring importance of immigration to the nation itself, to its broader history. Shteyngart's Vladimir at last is no dealer in trifling currency, no merely private little failure, but rather an exile whose allegiances in a dizzyingly cosmopolitan age remain profoundly and resonantly divided.

Given his parents' financial stability and his elite education, Vladimir would appear destined for upper-middle-class prosperity, yet his ambitions are complicated by his uneasiness with the consumption-driven, ahistorical life that defines conventional success in his adopted homeland. He feels he is in some sense imprisoned in the fantasies—and indeed in the "enlightened" liberal language—of affluent assimilated Americans, a predicament colorfully illustrated in his capitulation to his girlfriend Francesca's violent role-playing:

> The handkerchief was unfastened. Vladimir removed the blindfold himself. Rich Fifth Avenue light, healthy and dappled, overwhelmed the pale curtains.
>
> "Sorry about the coitus last night," Francesca said. "I was too rough. I was acting out."
>
> "No, it was my fault," Vladimir said, covering his lower quarters with sheets, rubbing his swollen wrists. . . . With a shaky finger, he traced the teeth marks inscribed on his upper thigh. "By physically acting out against me you became both aggrieved *and* perpetrator. You empowered yourself." These strange yet familiar words, unheard of since his tenure at the progressive Midwestern college, slipped out of his mouth.[22]

Shteyngart seems to parody and revise here Philip Roth's Alexander Portnoy, another insecure Jewish American male who seeks to confirm his manhood and sense of national belonging through erotic adventures with gentile women, or so-called shiksas: "What I'm saying, Doctor, is that I don't seem to stick my dick up these girls, as much as I stick it up their backgrounds—as though through fucking I will discover America. *Conquer* America—maybe that's more like it. Columbus, Captain Smith, Governor Winthrop, General Washington—now Portnoy."[23] Unlike his literary precursor, however, Vladimir cannot claim even temporary relief from identity crises in acting the role of sexual conquistador, and he will, until his departure from America, find himself unhappily cast in submissive roles.

The company of fellow immigrants, Vladimir laments, only confirms his failed assimilation: "He had no Russian friends. For all his years at the Emma Lazarus Society, the Russian community was just a dark, perspiring mass that regularly washed up on his shore, complaining, threatening, cajoling, bribing him with bizarre lacquered tea sets and bottles of Soviet champagne."[24] An alluring alternative looms for him, however, in the ostensible simplicity and backwardness of an *imagined* set of kinfolk, located for him in his parents' "sepia-toned Russia . . . a sooty and uncomfortable universe, but one with charms of its own."[25] In that recovered homeland, Vladimir feels, he might counter the deadening realities and vapid role-playing of U.S. capitalism: "the truth became obvious: state-sponsored socialism had been a good thing. Vladimir spent his waking hours daydreaming of the simple life of his parents. A walk along the Neva River with your intended: no charge. Box of stale chocolates and one wilted rose: fifty kopeks. Tickets for two to the Worker's Allegorical Puppet Theater: one ruble, ten kopeks (student rate). Now that was courtship! Empty wallets, empty stores, hearts filled with overflowing. . . . If only he and [Francesca] could travel back in time, away from the crude avarice of this uncultured metropolis, back to those tender Khrushchev nights."[26]

Natalie Friedman, in an astute consideration of the novel's relationship to works by other East European expatriate authors, and to the genre of American immigrant narratives more generally, rightly saw Shteyngart's America as a "land of anti-nostalgia or anti-memory," in which a "culture of upward mobility and promise of economic success conspire to repress the immigrant's memories of home."[27] Unlike those who, as "well-situated Americans," have already given up on such memories and can casually shuffle "through an endless catalog of social tendencies and intellectual poses," Vladimir feels pressured to resolve his dividedness: "He was twenty-five years old. Assimilate or leave, those were his options."[28] Though he experiments with a full commitment to acculturation—particularly in his relationship with Francesca, who epitomizes ethnic amnesia in her devotion to the endless possibilities of the American here and now—he remains nostalgic for, and yearns to escape to, the exotic alterity of an imagined Russian past.

In his parents Vladimir finds other nuanced negotiations of American mores and further confirmation of the vacuity of liberal idioms. His mother, a powerful corporate executive and the most dominant force in the family, remains attached to racial prejudices she acquired in Russia, though her religious affiliations are fluidly opportunistic:

> [Mother] lay in her mass-produced four-poster bed, nursing a bottle of rum, while Vladimir paced around her enormous berth lecturing on the topic of the day: Sensitivity to African-Americans. One black marketing director was about to be sacked, and Mother wanted to sack him "in the new, sensitive fashion."
>
> In the course of an hour, Vladimir pitted everything he learned during his stint at the progressive Midwestern college against Mother's peerless Russian racism. "So what are you telling me?" Mother said when the lesson was over. "I should bring up the middle passage?"
>
> . . .
>
> Vladimir accepted a glassful of rum. Mother grabbed a post and hoisted herself up until she was on her knees. "Jesus, our Lord," she said, "please

> shepherd helpless Vladimir away from his tragic lifestyle, from the legacy his father bequeathed him, from the pauper's flat which he calls home." She put her hands together but started to tip over.
>
> Vladimir caught her by one shoulder. "That's a pretty prayer, Mother," he said. "But we're, you know . . ." He lowered his voice out of habit: "*Jewish*."
>
> Mother looked at his face carefully, as if she had forgotten something and it had gone into hiding beneath one of Vladimir's thick brows. "Yes, I know that," she said, "but it's all right to pray to Jesus. Your grandfather was a gentile, you know, and his father was a deacon. And I still pray to the Jewish God, the main God, although, I have to say, he hasn't been helping much lately."[29]

Vladimir's father, a physician who has carved out a career based on "defrauding America's paradoxical health care system,"[30] escapes the material reality of America in his basement, which has been decorated to resemble scenes from his boyhood: "coarse off-white panels lining the walls were supposed to bring to mind the Russian birch; a set of unfinished wooden chairs gathered around a three-legged kitchen table bespoke an admirable poverty. On this table, there was some Pushkin, a little Lermontov. . . . The great warm stove, the centerpiece of his youth, was missing from the ensemble, but what could one do?"[31]

Vladimir's own sense of being *in* but not quite *of* the United States allows him, he feels, a certain moral liberation too, and he is attracted, partly because of his mother's humiliating goading, to the financial promises of criminality. After learning of the mafia empire led by a violent but charismatic man known as the Groundhog, he rationalizes his potential participation in it: "'Well,' Vladimir said. 'The story does raise some issues.' The Rule of Law, that bedrock of Western democracy—that was one issue. 'But we do have to remember,' Vladimir said, 'that we are poor Russians, that we live in difficult times for our homeland, and that we often have to take special measures to feed our families, to survive.'"[32] The speciousness of at least some of the rhetoric of ethnic victimization is a familiar refrain in *The Russian Debutante's Handbook,* and will become a thematic focus in *Absurdistan*.

Vladmir will propel himself back across the Atlantic, spurred by threats made by a gangster named Jordi, as well as his father's escapist fantasies of an Old World paradise and his mother's judgments of him as unmotivated, unmanly, and pathetically undisguised and unlikable as an ethnic Other: "'Vladimir,' she said, "you walk like a Jew.'"[33] A self-exile, "driven or thrust" (as in one sense of the Hebrew *garash*) away from one home, he will "expel" (as in another sense of *garash*) his second-rate status, remaking and restoring himself in exile: "From this day forward, he was Vladimir the Expatriate, a title that signified luxury, choice, decadence, frou-frou colonialism. Or, rather, Vladimir the Re-Patriate, in this case signifying a homecoming, a foreknowledge, a making of amends with history."[34]

Vladimir's dramatic self-affirmation abroad is appropriately and complexly ironic. He leaves his adopted homeland, the United States, where he was continually reminded of his foreign status,[35] for an imaginary "Russia," where he is taken for an authentic American. Though he has been a slacker in New York, the Russian mafia looks to him as an expert in hard-driving capitalism, and he convincingly sells himself to them—in P. T. Barnum-style—as the ultimate Yankee entrepreneur with just enough knowledge of the East to make himself seem credible to gullible Westerners. Moreover, by adopting the role of slick financial fraudster in Prava, Vladimir fulfils the demands of his mother for material success, becoming an "alpha immigrant" who makes good on the American dream, while conceiving of his schemes as, at least in part, a justified revenge on the spiritual emptiness of Americans and of global Americanization itself. He sets out "to plunder, to spoil," as in yet another sense of *garash:* "Amid the ghostly warble of old Soviet satellites circling over Prava, Mother [spoke to him]. *Proceed, my little treasure!* she said, *Take those uncultured bastards for all they're worth.*"[36]

The audacity of Vladimir's criminal plan brings to mind the schemes of Pavel Chichikov in Gogol's *Dead Souls.* A smooth-talking rogue who once partnered with organized criminals as a corrupt customs agent, Chichikov carries out his signature scam by traveling across the Russian countryside and buying up the titles of deceased serfs, with the aim of producing enough fraudulent collateral to pass for a wealthy landowner and secure a large government loan. Shteyngart seems to share with Gogol a presiding interest in satirizing so-called *poshlost,* a Russian word that carries a range of meanings but that can be roughly translated as "bad taste," "vulgarity," "presumptuous fakery," or, in its strongest shade, "devilish indecency." Common to most uses of the term is a sense of pretentious deception and inauthenticity—a "phoniness," as J. D. Salinger's Holden Caulfield might say—which seeks to pass off as real and valuable something that is not. Nabokov cited *poshlost* as a major focus of Gogol's work and noted that the concept includes "not only the obviously trashy but also the falsely important, the falsely beautiful, the falsely clever, the falsely attractive."[37] Chichikov, according to Nabokov, is a kind of universal embodiment of the darker shades of *poshlost,* "the ill-paid representative of the Devil, a traveling salesman from Hades, 'our Mr. Chichikov' as the Satan and Co. firm may be imagined calling their easygoing, healthy-looking but inwardly shivering and rotting agent."[38]

In his own assessment of Gogol's work, the Russian theologian Sergius Bulgakov drew a more chilling connection between *poshlost* and the Satanic, while similarly defining the concept as an insidious, soulless kind of playacting: "The beauty of Lucifer and the Demon that so enticed Byron and Lermontov is only a pose; it hides within itself deception and insipidness like expensive and luxurious secondhand clothing, worn over soiled linens, like a life luxuriating in debt and without any hope of repayment, like a dullard feigning genius. Beneath the demonic cloak are hidden Khlestikov [from Gogol's play *The Government Inspector*] and Chichikov; the fairy-like demon turns into a hideous devil with a hoof and a head-cold. Vulgarity [*poshlost*][39] is the hidden underbelly of demonism."[40] Both Gogol and Shteyngart explore ludicrous and sometimes grotesque characters whose *poshlost*—represented in their boorish behavior, trite attitudes, or kitschy style—typically has a strong, representative significance, suggesting a broader culture's toxic deceptiveness rather than that of any idiosyncratic individual (as Gogol's narrator challenges readers in *Dead Souls:* "And who among you, . . . in moments of solitary converse with himself, will point deeply into his own soul this painful question: 'And isn't there a bit of Chichikov in me, too?'")[41]

It also bears noting, when considering Shteyngart's relationship to Gogol here, the curiously "American" flavor of *Dead Souls*' themes. In a seminal assessment published in 1911, William Lyon Phelps contended that Chichikov, though clearly recognizable as Russian, nevertheless floats free of his immediate context and displays prominent affinities with a well-known American type: "No one can travel far in America without meeting scores of Chichikovs: indeed, he is an accurate portrait of the American promoter, of the successful commercial traveller, whose success depends entirely not on the real value and usefulness of his stock-in-trade, but on his knowledge of human nature and the persuasive power of his tongue. Chichikov is all things to all men."[42] Both Gogol and Shteyngart set imaginative sail for Russia but land, at least with one foot, on American soil.

Canonical American literature is full of works featuring slippery promoters and their conceptual kin. Among Vladimir's precursors can be counted, for instance, the silver-tongued King and Duke in Mark Twain's *Adventures of Huckleberry Finn*—and even the glib, socially evasive Huck himself—or the amoral entrepreneur Milo Minderbinder in Joseph Heller's satiric novel *Catch-22*. One is reminded here too of a Russian American precursor's infamous protagonist: Humbert Humbert, the lyrically self-justifying pedophile of Vladimir Nabokov's *Lolita* (1955). As Julian Moynahan pointed out in speculating on what drew Humbert from across the Atlantic, America—or more precisely, the *myth* of America—has long promised special opportunities to a certain class of freedom seeker: "For Europe, as first de Toqueville and then D. H. Lawrence expounded, America has figured as the place beyond cabined and confined traditions and sanctions. It has been the place where time itself might be redeemed, where the dream of a new Eden, of a second life, could be realized. Naturally, there has been a dark, pathological side to this. America has been the place indubitably attractive to great mischief makers, psychopaths, men on the run, unclubable and violent persons, con men."[43] The gangsters in *The Russian Debutante's Handbook*—who murder, extort, and generally terrorize those who obstruct their freewheeling enterprises—model, if comically, the sinister potential Moynahan identified, whereas mischievous Vladimir largely occupies the lighter side of such criminality. Both seem to suggest, however, something like the exploitation of a mythic American freedom, for they defy "cabined and confined traditions and sanctions" as they reinvent themselves in an Old World rapidly becoming New.

The prominence of this literary type, and its various permutations, has much to do with specific historical circumstances that have long shaped American life. In *The Confidence Man in American Literature* (1981), Gary Lindberg famously identified his titular figure as "a representative American"[44] who preys on the optimistic bent of the national character and exploits a set of fluid social conditions that make it difficult to discern the identities of those one meets. The con man, like Vladimir in Prava, embraces the challenge of taking on different roles in order to win the trust of others, and the more outlandish the role, the greater the pleasure in having convinced someone else of one's authenticity in performing it. The high levels of immigration to the United States throughout the nation's history, along with the mobility of its citizens once they have arrived, have meant that strangers must continually puzzle out one another's social coordinates as well as their own. What helps the con man in America, Lindberg claimed, is the tendency of Americans to *want* to believe in the promises of the strangers they meet:

> We can best understand the confidence man, then, through the characteristic situation in which he appears, a highly fluid situation with two special qualities. First, the continued movement of people has severed the connections between their appearances and their social positions. Their everyday practices no longer indicate their larger identities or their underlying values. All one can be sure of in such a situation is the immediate gesture, the technique itself. Thus the confidence man is surrounded by people who look hard and carefully at how one does something, who come to admire technical facility for its own sake. They have a how-to-do-it mentality. But there is another essential quality in the confidence man's situation: everyone

> around him believes in some larger promise. This collective attitude assures the manipulator that if he manages his immediate operations skillfully, the larger ends will take care of themselves. And of course this same promissory atmosphere makes people susceptible to transactions of faith. With this twofold situation in mind, we can begin to understand the confidence game as the practical making and manipulating of belief without substance for it.[45]

Vladimir is a sort of apprentice con man even before he heads to Prava, for his identity is an open question for him, a series of possibilities that he has in turn been trying to make believable not just to others but to himself.

Prava, Vladimir happily discovers, is full of credulous expatriates, fellow self-exiles who seek their own escape from America and yet discover an ironic return to it. In a running joke the city is dubbed the "Paris of the 90s,"[46] an imagined analogue to the artistic milieu that nourished expatriate geniuses—Ernest Hemingway, F. Scott Fitzgerald, Gertrude Stein, and others—in the early decades of the twentieth century. Vladimir notes with contempt the homogeneity of his fellow countrymen, white, middle-class, native-born twentysomethings who are complacently exploring life abroad before surrendering themselves to the bourgeoisie, and he soon learns to manipulate, in proper con man fashion, their willingness to believe in their own exceptional potential. As a cover for, and a satiric parallel to, his main swindle, he founds a literary journal that lures those with artistic ambitions: "It was all part of the familiar cultural Ponzi scheme practiced the world over—from third-rate dance collectives to those idiotic creative-writing programs. The participants put in their time and money, dutifully attended each other's kazoo recitals and poetry readings, and by the end of the day the only ingredient missing from their enterprise was the actual talent (much as a regular Ponzi scheme lacks the actual cash)."[47] Western *poshlost* is robustly satirized here, as the aspiring contributors display a posturing self-importance and self-delusion. Vladimir, who has resented being treated as something like an ethnic caricature in America among his liberal friends, now plays on their progressive sensibilities by creating a burlesqued version of his otherness, even going so far as to compose a poem about his "Russian mother in Chinatown," which he uses to "exoticize himself with as many ethnic references as possible."[48]

Vladimir's bogus company PravaInvest will exploit the political inclinations, moreover, of those who would redeem the lingering squalor of the East with the consumer comforts and "enlightened" orderliness of the West. In his pitch to the mobster known as the Groundhog, Vladimir skewers the naivety of American optimism as he positions PravaInvest as the kind of progressive, ecofriendly, well-regulated capitalist venture that his fellow expatriates would like to believe can be representative of the West's benign influence on developing nations. He depends, as Lindberg's archetypal con man always does, on an American faith in technical know-how, self-assurance, optimism about the future, and the plausibility of harmonizing idealism and greed:

> We make them feel like they're taking part in the resurgence of Eastern Europe. There's an American saying, spoken by a famous black man: "If you're not part of the solution, you're part of the problem." This saying has deep resonance in the American psyche, particularly among the liberal kind of American this city attracts. Now, we've got them not only becoming part of the solution but making money in the process. Or so they'll think. . . . It takes glossy brochures. We'll have to have them professionally made, not here, perhaps in Vienna. Oh, and we'll need artists' renderings of the five-star resort on Lake Boloto [Russian: "swamp"] that we're never going to build, and then an annual report featuring the smoky factories knocked down to make way for pleasant little corporate parks with recycling bins for glass and newspapers. . . . Sure, plenty of environmental stuff. That will sell. I see holistic centers and Reiki clinics, too.[49]

In Prava, Vladimir concludes, Americans pretend to have escaped their origins by experimenting with bohemian lifestyles, but ultimately project onto the city their own bright colonialist fantasies of a home away from home.

The shallow and presumptuous idealism of the American expatriate community (*poshlost* in another of its guises) is epitomized in the revolutionary dabbling of Morgan, Vladimir's girlfriend in Prava and eventual wife.[50] She harbors no plans for a long-term commitment to Stolovaya; she will, as it were, eat at this "canteen" and then casually depart. Feeling quite insulated from personal risk because of her American passport, she becomes involved in a plot to blow up the remains of a statue ("the Foot"[51]) symbolizing the city's communist past:

> "And nobody's going to get hurt, you know. The Foot's going to—" [said Morgan.]
>
> "I know, implode. I'm just a little worried about you. I mean, what if they catch you? Can you imagine yourself in a Stolovan jail? You've heard the *babushkas'* war cry. They'll send you to the gulag."
>
> Morgan narrowed her eyes in thought. She rubbed her mittens together. "But I'm an American," she said. She opened her mouth again, but there was nothing more to say on the subject.
>
> Vladimir absorbed her arrogance and even laughed a little. She was an American. It was her birthright to do as she pleased. "Besides," Morgan

> said, "*everybody* hates the Foot. The only reason it didn't get knocked down is because of official corruption. We're just doing what everyone wants. That's all."[52]

Morgan's involvement in this scheme would—like Francesca's erotic role-playing—channel her aggression in a dubious act of entitled empowerment. The "babushkas," who futilely but doggedly resist the city's transition to capitalism, are not counted in Morgan's effectively antidemocratic summation of the city's interests. In her unacknowledged colonial role, she would intervene in the fate of a culture she has failed to comprehend deeply. Shteyngart may have had in mind here William J. Lederer and Eugene Burdick's influential novel *The Ugly American* (1958),[53] for Morgan fits that work's titular stereotype, clumsily stalking communism abroad on behalf of what she takes to be universal values. Her neatly bipolar worldview is implied in the earnest question she poses to Vladimir before deciding to date him: "So, are you a good person?"[54] In Lederer and Burdick's narrative, American diplomats enter a fictional nation called Sarkkan, a version of Vietnam, in hopes of winning the political support of the local population but lose out to their Soviet counterparts because of their ignorance of—and essential indifference to—local customs. As one character in the novel remarks of American expatriates, "For some reason, the [American] people I meet in my country are not the same as the ones I knew in the United States. A mysterious change seems to come over Americans when they go to a foreign land. They isolate themselves socially. They live pretentiously. They are loud and ostentatious."[55]

Vladimir's partnership with the Groundhog involves a mutual confidence game, for he would have the mobster believe he is an authentic American entrepreneur (appropriately loud and ostentatious), while the Groundhog would have Vladimir believe that he is accepted as an authentic Russian or at least as a fellow Slav. Shteyngart's satirical descriptions of their meetings colorfully depict these con games, while also emphasizing with particular sharpness the ways in which the mafia seeks to emulate—in crude but nevertheless recognizable forms—the efficient exploitations of contemporary capitalism, producing their own versions of American ostentation:

> The Groundhog suddenly looked serious. "[Vladimir], let me speak from the heart. You and Kostya are the future of this organization. I see that now. Before it was fun, sure, run around, blow up a few diners, cut off some dicks, but we got to get serious. This is the nineties. We're in this . . . 'informational age' . . . we need 'Americanisms' and 'globalisms.' Do you know where I'm coming from?"

> "Oh, yes," Vladimir said. "I say we call a meeting, the whole organization."
> "Whores and all," said the Groundhog.
> "We're going to teach them America."
> "*You're* going to teach them America."
> "Me?" Vladimir said, swallowing a cognac.
> "You," the Groundhog said.
> "Me?" Vladimir feigned surprise yet again.
> "You're the best."
> "No, you're the best."
> "No, you."
> What happened next was as good an argument for temperance as any. "You're the top," Vladimir sang, squeezing in a shot of pear brandy between the lyrics. "You're the Colosseum."
> He must have been louder than he thought, for the pianist instantly shifted out of his Dr. Zhivago repertoire and struck up Vladimir's tune. The pianist was, like nearly everyone in Prava, open to suggestions.[56]

The Cole Porter song invoked here—"You're the Top," from the 1930s musical *Anything Goes*—wittily suggests Eastern Europe's postcommunist romance with Western influences, given that the original lyrics involve a series of mutual compliments, while bringing the moral status of those influences into question. Shteyngart gestures here toward the brutality of "legitimate" capitalist practices, a theme he explores more deeply in *Absurdistan* and *Super Sad True Love Story.* He further suggests the practical equivalence of respectable corporate executives and an execrated criminal class. As Vladimir asks himself, remembering his mother's exhortations to follow her path to American riches, "Would she be proud? Would she consider his little pyramid scheme a cheap alternative to an MBA? Has he inadvertently created something that will please her? Come to think of it, is there really any difference between Mother's corporate colossus and his scrappy PravaInvest?"[57]

If such scenes offer critiques of Western capitalism by likening it to criminality, others seem to use the mafia to highlight the broader decadence of the post-Soviet era while also perhaps toying with Western perceptions of that decadence. The novel's satire blooms most colorfully—and no doubt, for many Russian readers, most offensively—in its representations of these figures' sensational vulgarity or extreme *poshlost,* approaching something like the comic grotesques for which Gogol is celebrated. As Svetlana Boym noted, nineteenth-century Russian intellectuals often used the term *poshlost* to describe as well as condemn tasteless Russian mimicry of Western culture.[58] Vladimir confronts the mafia's poor imitation of Western fashions in the twenty-first century as he attempts to upgrade their air of professionalism while inculcating his own versions of *poshlost* business practices. In one spirited act of aesthetic sanitization, he has his partners strip down their appallingly decorated cars: "Out came the zebra-striped seats, the wooly cup holders, the shocking Electric Plum ground effects—all tossed water-brigade style past a line of bobbing blond heads and into the circle of the clearing. There, the personal offerings to the God of Kitsch were already assembled: the nylon tracksuits, the Rod Stewart compilations, the worn Romanian sneakers, everything that had qualified the Groundhog's vast crew as Easterners, Soviets, Cold War-losers—all would be kindling for the flames."[59]

Multiple senses of *garash* are at play here, for as a mentor to the Russians, Vladimir has sought to refine their larcenous potential, helping them exploit newly available opportunities without restraint: "Therefore thus says the Lord GOD: 'Surely I have spoken in My burning jealousy against the rest of the nations and against all Edom, who gave My land to themselves as a possession, with wholehearted joy and spiteful minds, in order to plunder [*migrash,* from the root *garash*] its open country'" (Ezekiel 36:5, NKJV). Agitated by a sense of unbelonging, Vladimir has immersed himself in sordid criminality, while attempting to drive out the worst of the Russians' roiling appropriations of the West ("But the wicked are like the troubled [*garash*] sea, when it cannot rest, whose waters cast up [*garash*] mire and dirt" [Isaiah 57:20, KJV]).

Poshlost, as Boym interpreted it, "is the Russian version of banality, with a characteristic national flavoring of metaphysics and high morality, and a peculiar conjunction of the sexual and the spiritual."[60] Shteyngart has offered vivid sketches of its contemporary manifestation in Russian sexual depravity, but perhaps none is so vivid as the Groundhog's description to Vladimir of how he met "the love of his life, Lenochka"[61] in a brothel:

> "So Groundhog is leaving House of Girl, but then he hearing beautiful sound from room of love. 'Okh! Okh! Okh!' It is like wonderful Slavic angel. 'Okh! Okh! Okh!' Voice tender like young girl. 'Okh! Okh! Okh!' He is asking Madame: 'Tell me, who is making Okh?' Madame is saying, oh, is our Lenochka making such Okh, but she is only for *valuta,* for, you know, hard currency. Groundhog is, like: 'I have dollar, Deutsche mark, Finnish markka, *nu,* what you want?' So Madame is saying, okay, sit down on divan for twenty minutes and soon you will have this Lena.' So Groundhog sitting and sitting and he is hearing this beautiful 'okh' sound like bird singing to another bird, and he is suddenly becoming, eh . . . How do you say, Vladimir?"

> He whispered a word in Russian. "Well . . . Engorged, I guess," Vladimir translated, softening the hard meaning a bit.[62]

Such scenes are characteristic of the novel's playfulness with ethnic clichés—suggesting an indulgence in stereotypes of the hopelessly debauched post-Soviet era for wild comic effect but perhaps also, more subtly, an ironic meta-commentary on the distorted quality of the West's imagination of the ostensibly barbaric East.[63]

Vladimir's paradoxical "re-patriation" in Prava seems to satisfy his yearning for a satisfying identity for a time. Before their violent breakup, he comes to feel a profound kinship with the gangsters with whom he partners: he "looked to the Russians sitting before him. . . . They smoked too much, drank too much, killed too much. They spoke a dying language and, to be honest, were themselves not too long for this world. *They were his people.* Yes, after thirteen years in the American desert, Vladimir Girshkin had stumbled upon a different kind of tragedy. A better place to be unhappy. He had finally found his way home."[64] In spite of the rapid changes that are transforming Eastern Europe after the fall of Communism, including the rise of new and brutal criminal networks, Vladimir claims to detect there a cultural gravity signifying something like the perfect antidote to his weightless New World experience. Prava—again, "right" or "correct" in Russian—promises him, in contrast to America's meretricious insistence on the shallow present, a set of cultural "ingredients" deemed to be "primordial, essential, revelatory."[65] This partly ironic epiphany is linked in a subtle intertextual nod to another canonical American novel featuring a tragically nostalgic con man. Just as F. Scott Fitzgerald's Jay Gatsby[66] "believed in the *green light,* the orgastic future that year by year recedes before us"[67] (emphasis added), Shteyngart's Vladimir finds in the communist remnants of Prava a portentous, if declining, emerald emblem: "The truth was that for the last twenty years, from Soviet kindergarten to the Emma Lazarus Immigrant Absorption Society, all the signs had been pointing to this ravine, these *panelaks* [panel buildings], this sinking green moon."[68]

The "babushkas"—the Stolovayan women who defend "the Foot" and cling to the moral certainties of their nation's Soviet past—strike Vladimir as plain but nevertheless alluring reflections of that green light, even as he pursues a lifestyle diametrically opposed to theirs. Compared to his own uncertainties about who or even where he is, these women seem to him untroubled by questions of self-identity in spite of their status as disesteemed historical relics. The new capitalist order may have left them behind, but that is their virtue: they do not agonize in deciding who they are or might become but instead commit themselves to defending a fixed, traditional set of ideals. In these "right" or "correct" women of Prava, Vladimir locates an imaginatively compelling alternative, however marginal and beleaguered, to capitalist exploitation and decadence. As Nataša Kovačević contended, for Vladimir "the traces of communism [in Prava] recall a failed and ugly dream, but one that was also the dream of social empowerment and equality. They introduce a memory . . . of a different way of being, of a space not yet swamped with multinational corporations buying off the country, a populace not yet widely impoverished and a time before commodity consumption becomes a pastime for the select few."[69] The presence of a communist holdover thus confirms Vladimir's nostalgia for a "sepia-toned Russia" as well as the supposed promise of ethnic belonging that goes with it, which is not quite dispatched by the garish tones of the post-Soviet era. Nevertheless the appearance of these communist "traces" is framed by obvious ironies. Vladimir's own time in Prava is spent in greedy pursuit of riches and the heady consumption of a range of commodities licit and illicit, and he shows little interest in actually participating in the supposed simplicity of the precapitalist era. Moreover, the babushkas are themselves more than faintly ridiculous in their blind adherence to outdated mores, and, no matter how much Vladimir sentimentalizes them, they seem to epitomize yet another version, if a marginal and moribund one, of the falseness of *poshlost*.

In spite of his attraction to Prava's representatives of old and new social orders, Vladimir ultimately confronts the impossibility of making the East his permanent home. After mutual betrayals, the Groundhog turns on him, and he must flee the city in order to escape being killed. An intractable barrier to his Eastern assimilation, he comes to realize, is not his "American" past, which he has been successfully leveraging, but his outsider status as a Jew. As Olga Gershenson and David Schneer explained, Jews were categorized in Soviet times as a distinct nationality, and they remain stigmatized in the post-Soviet era according to notions of intractable physical differences:

> In some ways, Jewish identity in the Soviet Union was very much fixed. Jews were identified first by their passports, which clearly defined their ethnicity (*natsional'nost'* in Russian) as Jewish. Even today, with that rubric in passports gone, experience suggests that Russian Jews are seen by others and see themselves as ethnically, even biologically, different. Allegedly, they can be identified by their body type, noses, gait, hair, and skin color. As Soviet literary representations and testimonials show, Jewishness is deeply embodied.[70]

In other words Vladimir may play at being Russian, but his Russian peers see through that performance to some underlying form of difference or even inferiority. An openly anti-Semitic mobster named Gusev continually reminds

Vladimir that his ultimate ethnic identification can only be "Jew," not Russian, and, more dramatically, a group of racist skinheads viciously attack him, first on their own and then at the mafia's behest, after identifying his skin tone and facial features as signs of racial otherness.

Vladimir notes that while both Russians and Jews have repeatedly and notoriously been victims of historical trauma, those belonging to both categories are singled out for special abuse:

> A knowledgeable Russian lazing around in the grass, sniffing clover and munching on boysenberries, expects that at any minute the forces of history will drop by and discreetly kick him in the ass.
>
> A knowledgeable Jew in a similar position expects history to spare any pretense and kick him directly in the face.
>
> A *Russian Jew* (knowledgeable or not) expects both history *and* a Russian to kick him in the ass, face, and every other place where a kick can be reasonably lodged.[71]

Vladimir's response to the forbidding weight of history is to prepare himself against the likelihood of abuse: "His take on the matter was: Victim, stop lazing about in the grass."[72] Moreover, one of his complaints against his Jewish American companion, a midwesterner named Perry Cohen, is that he is much too complacent about the privileges he has been afforded as a native-born citizen; Russian Jews, insists Vladimir, actually know what oppression is: he "was ready to attack Cohen with his own background, from the Jew-baiting of Leningrad to his years as a Stinky Russian Bear in Westchester. Assimilation, my ass. What do *you* know of assimilation, spoiled American pig? Why, I'll show you. . . . I'll show you all!"[73] Whereas Perry has been spared any emphatic experience of social marginalization, Vladimir cannot forget his own history of persecution in both his original and adopted homes, and he feels haunted by a kind of predestined victimhood, which is once again an indication of his name-fate as a "driven, agitated" soul. His departure from the Soviet Union was, it is revealed, accompanied by the bullying anti-Semitism of agents of the Interior Ministry who insultingly predicted his family's return: "As they tore through Mother's address book, shredding anything with an American address, including her Newark cousin's instructions on how to get to Macy's, a particularly large gentleman, whom Vladimir would never forget as having had a mouth frighteningly empty of teeth (even the silver kind that were standard issue to middle-aged Warsaw Pact citizens) and a strong smell of sturgeon on his breath, said to her: You'll be back, Yid.'"[74]

After visiting Auschwitz-Birkenau, Vladimir is reminded, moreover, of the grim history that motivated his ancestors' flight from Russia generations earlier: his grandmother "had escaped the gas and the bombs, investing body and soul in the Soviet system that ultimately took as many lives as the Teutonic evil streaming through the borders in columns of panzer and precision-strafing from above. Her lesson to Vladimir was as clear as it should have been for his fellow Jews interned in the pond of ashes down the track: *Get out while you can and by any means necessary.* Run, before the *goyim* get you, and get you they will, no matter . . . how much they claim to love you while the absinthe flows."[75] In a novel so full of con men and con games, false appearances and false declarations, *this* advice—and the weight of the historical catastrophe from which it surfaces—comes closest to affixing the narrative world in the real, providing a kind of moral ballast to Vladimir's swaying, illusory panorama of West and East. Its borrowing of a famous phrase—Malcolm X's "by any means necessary"—is repeated in *Absurdistan* as part of an acerbic representation of the contemporary status of ethical ideals.

Shteyngart's representation of Jewishness in the novel has, however, often come under attack. Adam Rovner contended that Shteyngart's representation of a "vulnerable, ineffectual, anxious" protagonist indulges in a damaging ethnic stereotype—the schlemiel—suggesting "all that remain are enervated visions of Jewishness: the Jew as sad sack, sexual bumbler, or comic *tummler.* Such representations lack deep cultural, historical, or religious affiliation. Jews are figured as different, but harmlessly so."[76] Morris Dickstein argued in a similar vein that Vladimir's Jewishness becomes visible from a series of negative characteristics: "He experiences himself as a Jew only in his sense of marginality, or when he sees himself as schlemiel-like, inept, physically clumsy, or when he's cursed out as a Jew, or begins an affair with a wholesome American girl."[77] Jesper Reddig suggested that Vladimir's wooing of, and eventual marriage to, Morgan—though self-consciously pitched as a cliché—nevertheless represents a kind of surrender to the American racial hierarchy: "In a sense, Morgan's whiteness is unbearable insofar as it proves irresistible to Vladimir: even as it is carried out under the disguise of spoof hybridity and through a gesture of ironic critical distance, Shteyngart allegorically replays turn-of-the-century Jewish ethnic choice—in his carefully composed narrative pattern, his protagonist, in the end, embraces the whiteness paradigm."[78]

Vladimir is last seen in "good old Cleveland,"[79] where he suppresses the spiritual "cleft" in his identity and "cleaves" to his gentile wife, as well as to the comforts and mundane rewards of midwestern mediocrity. This destination perhaps puns on Genesis 2:24—"Therefore shall a man leave his father and his mother, and shall cleave unto his wife: and they shall be one flesh"—as Vladimir in fact fulfills his parents' ambitions for him, "returning" to their favor by settling in to an assimilated American life, with, no less, a shiksa bride, whom his mother approves of while wishing "she were a little blonder."[80] After the fantastical tumult of his time abroad, he now aspires, he tells us, to "the simple brotherhood of America's white men."[81] Driving to work each morning "in the plush cocoon of his luxury utility vehicle," he will imbibe Eastern *poshlost* in measured, homeopathic doses, "listening to the scratchy wail of the Russian bard Vladimir Vysotsky—it is his favorite morning song, set in a Soviet mental asylum where the inmates have just discovered the mystery of the Bermuda Triangle on a television variety show and are full of disturbing suggestions."[82]

The lure of the exotic still haunts Vladimir, however, and his fantasies sometimes carry him off to distant locales: "A scheme! A provocation! Pyramids! Turbo props! The Frankfurt exchange! The old Girshkin something for nothing!"[83] One thinks here of Tennyson's Ulysses, another divided, ambivalent figure who after extraordinary adventures rests uneasily among an unromantic people:

> It little profits that an idle king,
> By this still hearth, among these barren crags,
> Match'd with an aged wife, I mete and dole
> Unequal laws unto a savage race,
> That hoard, and sleep, and feed, and know not me.
> I cannot rest from travel: I will drink
> Life to the lees: All times I have enjoy'd
> Greatly, have suffer'd greatly, both with those
> That loved me, and alone, on shore, and when
> Thro' scudding drifts the rainy Hyades
> Vext the dim sea: I am become a name[84]

Vladimir too has somewhat unhappily "become a name"[85]—not a famous one, but merely his name-fate, a self-exiled Girshkin, "cast out [*garash*] and drowned as by the flood of Egypt" (Amos 8:8). And just as Tennyson's Ulysses contemplates the domesticated life of Telemachus, Vladimir imagines the future status of his own son, who will be spared the agitated process of assimilation, "free of the fear and madness of Vladimir's Eastern lands . . . [an] American in America."[86]

CHAPTER 3

Absurdistan

By the time Shteyngart published his second novel in 2006, he was, owing to the success of *The Russian Debutante's Handbook*, already an international literary celebrity. *Absurdistan* is in part a response to that celebrity, and its ironies are more self-conscious and complex than those of its precursor—above all, of course, in relation to representations of Russian and Jewish identities.

Absurdistan chronicles the attempts of a thirty-year-old, 325-pound Jewish Russian émigré named Misha Vainberg, graduate of a midwestern liberal arts college and heir to the fortune of a ruthless oligarch-gangster, to return from Eastern Europe to his lover, Rouenna Sales, in New York City. Standing in his way is the Immigration and Naturalization Service, which has banished him after discovering that his father has murdered an Oklahoma business rival. Misha's adventures take him to Absurdsvanï (Absurdistan), an oil-rich, former-Soviet republic now inelegantly transitioning to capitalism, where he seeks a Belgian passport from a corrupt government official.[1] In naming his protagonist "Misha," Shteyngart gestured, perhaps, to the popular bear mascot used by the Soviet Union to promote the 1980 Summer Olympic Games. Misha has, it is revealed, sometimes been treated like a sort of ethnic symbol in America, more a compendium of clichés than an individual. His last name, "Vainberg," seemingly implies his status as an idle mountain (German: *berg*), an emblem of narcissistic accumulation.

Much of the thematic territory covered in *Absurdistan* will be familiar to readers of Shteyngart's first novel: the rise of an obscenely wealthy and corrupt oligarchy in Russia and Eastern Europe, the leveling and deadening cultural effects of globalization, the sprawling and sinister influence of transnational corporations, the limits of and prejudices lurking within Euro-American multiculturalism, the tensions inherent in constructing a Russian Jewish identity, and the ultimate, uncanny incommensurability of Russian and American ways of life. The novels' protagonists also have a good deal in common; in fact Vladimir Girshkin makes several appearances in *Absurdistan* during flashbacks. Both characters are young, Jewish Russian émigrés from families who have flourished financially through ethically questionable means. Both attended Accidental College, where they were steeped in liberal ideology, and both struggle with the triangulation of their Russian, Jewish, and American identities. Yet there is a kind of mirror play going on here too. Vladimir dreams of leaving America for the East and does so, whereas Misha dreams of returning to America from the East but cannot. Vladimir is uncomfortable with his Americanization; Misha embraces it. Vladimir is bullied by his mother, who wants him to appear less Jewish and complete his assimilation; Misha is manipulated by his father, who would have him embrace Judaism and confirm his status as an outsider in both America and Russia.

Reviews of *Absurdistan* were largely positive, and the work was ultimately cited as one of the best novels of the year by the *New York Times* and the *Washington Post,* among other publications, further elevating Shteyngart's critical status (nevertheless, like *The Russian Debutante's Handbook,* it was received unfavorably in Russia).[2] Writing in the *New York Times,* Walter Kirn offered high praise for Shteyngart, whom he likened to the novel's protagonist, as above all a stylist:

> Shteyngart and Misha, exuberant depressives, don't stint on the syntax or the verbiage when objects huge and rotten hulk into view. Their thick, overloaded style is what happens, though, when socialist realism decays into black comedy. This is the prose of heroic disappointment, faintly labored at moments but fitted to the task of shoveling up mountains of cultural debris. Hemingway's clean sentences wouldn't do here. A man needs commas, semicolons, adjectives. He requires linguistic heavy machinery.[3]

Laura Miller's review in Salon.com invoked Joseph Heller and complimented the sharpness of the novel's vision of the former Soviet bloc: "No doubt Shteyngart's portrait of life in Russia and the 'stans' is equally acute, no matter how exaggerated it seems. Like Heller's *Catch-22, Absurdistan* has the feel of a book whose outrageous caricatures will soon become shorthand for real-life situations. We're all Absurdistanis, or will be soon."[4] Turning to another American precursor, Patrick Ness cited John Kennedy Toole's *A Confederacy of Dunces* as the novel's "closest spiritual brother," and praised its "surprisingly sensuous" satire.[5] Aleksandar Hemon made a by now common comparison to a Russian literary master: "*Absurdistan* is not just a hilarious novel, but also a record of a particular peak in the history of human folly. No one is more capable of dealing with the transition from the hell of socialism to the hell of capitalism in Eastern Europe than Shteyngart, the great-great-grandson of one Nikolai Gogol and the funniest foreigner alive."[6]

Recent critical studies of *Absurdistan* have focused on the novel's satirical representation of identity politics, particularly its probing of contemporary Jewish identity. Steven S. Lee compared Shteyngart's representation of an Eastern outsider in America with Sacha Baron Cohen's character Borat, who starred in a popular film the same year *Absurdistan* was published. As Lee concluded, "*Borat* and *Absurdistan* similarly present cultural tolerance as a mask for enduring prejudice and inequality."[7] Dean J. Franco assessed the novel in light of other contemporary works by Jewish American authors and argued for its ultimate cynicism about essential foundations of belonging: "Shteyngart gives his readers a politics that is always against ethics, religion drained of spirituality, territory that has too much religion."[8] Olga Gershenson and David Schneer suggested that Shteyngart "emerges as a cultural translator between different kinds of Jews: between Russian Jews at home and Russian Jews 'in exile,' and between Americans and new immigrants,"[9] while Adrian Wanner contended that "the expression of an alleged national or ethnic authenticity turns in Shteyngart's fiction into a self-conscious ironic pastiche."[10]

In *Nothing Is True and Everything Is Possible,* journalist Peter Pomerantsev described the rise of capital in Russia about a decade after the fall of the Soviet Union:

> In the twenty-first century, something happened: money. Never had so much money flowed into so small a place in so short a time. The orbital system shifted. . . . The Russians were the new jet set: the richest, the most energetic, the most dangerous. They had the most oil, the most beautiful women, the best parties. From being ready to sell anything, they became ready to buy anything: football clubs in London and basketball clubs in New York; art collections, English newspapers, and European energy companies. No one could understand them. They were both lewd and refined, cunning and naive.[11]

Misha Vainberg's father, the oligarch-gangster Boris Vainberg, is part of this new class of wealthy Russians, and he suggests, like the Mafiosi in *The Russian Debutante's Handbook,* the ultimate equivalence of Eastern organized crime with the routine, if better disguised, practices of Western capitalism.[12] Jailed in the 1980s for "dissident Zionist activities,"[13] he ingeniously transformed himself into a successful profiteer after being released into the post-Soviet world. If American "multiculturalism" maintains a certain innocence about capitalism, Boris is fully aware of its brutal realities, and he cannily partners with other ambitious impresarios eager to exploit opportunities in the "wild East": "All those Georgians and Tatars and Ukrainians with the sweaty-brow entrepreneurial spirit so beloved by the American consulate. All the Inguish and Ossetians and Chechans with the casual attitude toward public violence that would create the fine explosive Russia we know today. These men could throw a punch, strangle a hooker, fake a customs form, hijack a truck, blow up a restaurant, start a shell company, buy a television network, run for parliament. Oh, they were *kapitalists,* all right."[14]

Misha, as the pampered son of Boris, is not asked to do much at all in the way of capitalist accumulation, and it falls to him instead to be an exuberant cosmopolitan consumer, a well-placed—if not always well-informed—observer of the processes of globalization. Though he notes his impression, as a Russian American, of "the logical impossibility of a place like Russia existing alongside the civilized world,"[15] he also emphasizes the ways in which his homeland's traditional charms have been corrupted as it transitions into something like a faltering, *poshlost* caricature of the West. The architectural grandeur of St. Petersburg, for instance, has been marred by sprawling slums and the plaguelike spread of transnational commercialism:

> [The city] has taken on the appearance of a phantasmagoric third-world city, our neoclassical buildings sinking into the crap-choked canals, bizarre peasant huts fashioned out of corrugated metal and plywood colonizing the broad avenues with their capitalist iconography (cigarette ads featuring an American football player catching a hamburger with a baseball mitt), and what is worst of all, our intelligent, depressive citizenry has been replaced by a new race of mutants dressed in studied imitation of the West, young women in tight Lycra, their scooped-up little breasts pointing at once to New York and Shanghai, with men in fake black Calvin Klein jeans hanging limply around their caved-in asses.[16]

In Absurdsvanï, Misha discovers more extreme polarities in wealth distribution, with the poor living in squalor and the upwardly mobile indulging in fervent simulations of American fashions. As Nabokov defined it, the strain of *poshlost* discernible in the latter group has to do with a gritty venality, its practitioners seemingly convinced that "the acme of human happiness is purchasable, and that its purchase somehow ennobles the purchaser."[17] The basic, ignoble dynamic between the haves and have-nots is, the novel implies, effectively one of prostitution, with foreign powers extracting the nation's only valuable commodity, oil, while reserving most of the economic benefits for themselves and a small local elite. In the capital city's Hyatt Hotel, sex workers underscore this impression by soliciting American oil executives poolside, while fanning themselves hopefully with the *Financial Times*. As Alfred J. López remarked, "the aftermath of each of the global cataclysms of the last decade have amply illustrated [that] it is the poor, the disenfranchised and marginalized who are most vulnerable to the vicissitudes of increasingly volatile global markets and bear the brunt of the suffering when things inevitably go wrong";[18] Shteyngart, affirmed López, in linking *Absurdistan* with Monica Ali's *Brick Lane* and Kiran Desai's *The Inheritance of Loss,* succeeded "in portraying the polyglot dystopia of the postglobal world because [he foregrounded] those subjects most immediately impacted by it."[19]

In its representation of the conditions of global capitalism, the novel teasingly deploys a range of ethnic caricatures—especially, as above, Russian ones. The book opens with a dedication made "with that cloying Russian affection that passes for real warmth,"[20] moves on to a thumbnail sketch of "a nation of busybody peasants thrust into an awkward modernity,"[21] then offers periodic invocations of a people's collective melancholy and fatalism over the next several hundred pages. Much as he did in *The Russian Debutante's Handbook*—though here with more coyness and complexity—Shteyngart has presented a burlesque of Russian character, along with Russian and American ways of *conceiving* that character, giving us a series of comic identities that nevertheless lay claim to some essential plausibility. When Misha sums up his countrymen's spirituality with the cynical judgement that "some of us are believers . . . but mostly we just want things"[22] or despairs that "*Nothing will ever come of this land,*"[23] the ironies here allow for a withering critique of the demoralized conditions of post-Soviet life, along with a distancing acknowledgement that such critiques are themselves a function of excessive melancholy and fatalism and as such are partly distortive and inadequate.

The novel's playfulness with ethnicity extends to Misha's self-affiliation with what seems like the entirety of the Russian literary canon. In framing the novel according to his narrator's rhetorical appeal to the Immigration and Naturalization Service, Shteyngart wryly addressed, perhaps, his own broader public, with whom he is half-seriously attempting to establish claims to both Russian and American identities: "As you read about my life and struggles in these pages, you will see certain similarities with Oblomov, the famously large gentleman who refuses to stir from his couch in the nineteenth-century novel [by Ivan Goncharov] of the same name. . . . [And] may I suggest another possibility: Prince Myshkin from Dostoyevsky's *The Idiot*. Like the prince, I am something of a holy fool."[24] Though allusions to Goncharov and Dostoevsky are most frequent in the novel, a pantheon of past masters is cited along the way, as if cueing book reviewers looking for flattering comparisons: among them, Turgenev, Lermontov, Tolstoy, Chekhov, Gogol, Babel, and Nabokov. Once again, of course, Shteyngart's irony insinuates both a closeness to, and a metatextual distance from, the literature being invoked. He invites readers to note family resemblances that would place the novel firmly within a Russian literary genealogy, while winking at the presumptuousness of that invitation as well as the temptation to collapse the work of an ostensibly exotic "immigrant author" into clichéd notions of what is most authentically Russian. Misha is an exuberant global citizen of the twenty-first century, yet he travels with a "manservant" who is treated like a serf, and often filters his world through the lens of classic literary constructions (including non-Russian ones, as in Misha's remark—which would just as surely apply to himself and his manservant—that two gangsters resemble Cervantes' Don Quixote and Sancho Panza).[25] For instance, in one section he moves from commenting on a murder caught on videotape, the prevalence of contemporary designer drugs, and a newscaster's joke about Chernobyl, to noting that a man reminds him of "one of Gogol's crafty peasants."[26] The effect is to suggest similarity and difference simultaneously, aligning the novel with a distinguished tradition while also displacing that alignment: "In a novel written during the golden age of Russian literature, a man named Svyokla would look like a *svyokla,* that is to say, he would be red as a beet. But in the era of modern produce, Colonel Svyokla's head resembled a giant genetically modified peach, fraudulently spherical and ripe, the skin dry and crisp."[27]

Shteyngart's self-referential jesting becomes even more intricate in the novel's allusions to *The Russian Debutante's Handbook*—Vladimir Girshkin turns out to have been a college acquaintance of Misha's—and in the introduction of an ironic doppelgänger, Jerry Shteynfarb, who is apparently the odious embodiment of criticisms launched at the actual author since his emergence as a literary celebrity.[28] The most nagging of these, of course, concerns Shteyngart's claim to "Russianness" and the impression he has sometimes given of acting as a cynical ethnic self-promoter. Adrian Wanner, in a trenchant discussion of the identity politics involved in the marketing of the author's work, reported that in a radio interview (in Russian) Shteyngart "declared that it was his conscious intention to introduce the Russian element into the genre of American immigrant literature—almost as if he were presenting his ethnicity as a potentially profitable brand in a currently fashionable market niche."[29] According to Misha, Shteynfarb's career is based on nothing more than hucksterism, a shrewd exploitation of the marketability of his ethnicity:

> He had been a schoolmate of mine at Accidental College, a perfectly Americanized Russian émigré (he came to the States as a seven-year-old) who managed to use his dubious Russian credentials to rise through the

> ranks of the Accidental creative writing department and to sleep with half the campus in the process. After graduation, he made good on his threat to write a novel, a sad little dirge about his immigrant life, which seems to me the luckiest kind of life imaginable. I think it was called *The Russian Arriviste's Hand Job* or something of the sort. The Americans, naturally, lapped it up.[30]

Though Misha admits to having benefitted from his own leveraging of an exotic Russian identity, he bitterly accuses Shteynfarb, who seduces, impregnates, and abandons Rouenna, of "playing the professional immigrant game"[31] as he advances a literary career based on writing "unfunny short stories chronicling the differences between Russians and Americans."[32] In a related gesture toward the cynical production of ethnic "authenticity," Shteyngart has noted how a character named Larry Zartarian, a California-raised manager of an Absurdsvanï hotel catering to Westerners, carefully crafts the broken English of his notes to guests in order to fulfil their expectations of charming ethnic otherness.[33] These moments of self-satire allow Shteyngart to broach—and perhaps, to some extent, concede the legitimacy of—concerns about the authenticity of his own Russian credentials and the canniness of his self-promotion, while also playfully distancing himself from them and thus ostensibly outflanking his critics.[34]

One Russian literary precursor whose themes do seem genuinely at play in *Absurdistan*—far more than Goncharov's *Oblomov,* in spite of that work's repeated invocations—is Ivan Turgenev's *Fathers and Sons.* Both novels are concerned with dramatizing generational conflicts brought on by profound cultural shifts—and in particular by intellectual fashions that have drifted into the Russian world from the West and been assumed by the *poshlost* avant-garde. In Turgenev's novel, a young man named Bazarov and his friend Arkady offer spirited, if callow, challenges to the traditional moral bearings of their elders:

> "He is a nihilist," repeated Arkady.
>
> "A nihilist," said Nikolai Petrovich. "That's from the Latin *nihil, nothing,* so far as I can judge. Therefore, the word denotes a man who . . . who doesn't recognize anything?"
>
> "Say, rather, who doesn't respect anything," added Pavel Petrovich and once more busied himself with the butter.
>
> "Who approaches everything from a critical point of view," remarked Arkady.
>
> "Isn't that the same thing?"
>
> "No, it's not the same thing. A nihilist is a man who doesn't acknowledge

> any authorities, who doesn't accept a single principle on faith, no matter how much that principle may be surrounded by respect."
>
> "And that's a good thing, is it?" interjected Pavel Petrovich.
>
> "It depends on who you are, uncle. It's a good thing for one man and a bad thing for another."
>
> "Is that so! Well, I can see it's not for us. We, men of another age, we suppose that without . . . [principles] accepted, as you put it, on faith we can't take a single step, we can't even breathe."[35]

Misha—an outsized figure but nonetheless a representative of contemporary "youth culture"—can also be thought of as a kind of ironic inversion of Turgenev's callow nihilists, for he is an "omnist" in his affirmation of a teeming diversity of "principles" and is just as mistaken as Bazarov in understanding exactly where his deepest sympathies lie. Having adopted an American liberal ethos, he professes, in ultimate defiance of his father's insistence that he'll "always be a Jew,"[36] a broad respect for—and identification with—multiple traditions and their specific claims.

In fact the central satirical focus of *Absurdistan* seems to fall on Misha's and others' pluralist pretensions and their collision with traditional orthodoxies. The sociologist Zygmunt Bauman articulated a critique of the excessively *un*discriminating and all-consuming bent of "the multicultural age" that seems largely parallel to Shteyngart's construction of his protagonist's professed ideals: "[Its] proclamation . . . [is] a declaration of intent: of a refusal to pass judgement and to take a stand; a declaration of indifference, of hands being washed of petty quarrels about preferred styles of life or favorite values. It displays the new "cultural omnivorousness" of the global elite: let's treat the world as a gigantic department store with shelves full of the most varied offers, and let's be free to roam one floor after another, try and taste every item on display, pick them up to our heart's desire."[37] Misha's mountainous stature indeed suggests his symbolic status as a cosmopolitan omnivore, bloated not just by the consumption of luxury goods that his inheritance bequeaths him, but by the celebratory absorption of cultural multitudes. Having been educated, like Vladimir Girshkin and Shteyngart himself, at an elite liberal arts college in the Midwest, he has gorged, as it were, on a progressive American inclusiveness. His degree is in "Multicultural Studies," a discipline that the novel mocks for its naive championing of the "outsider" and celebration of any and all cultural differences. In a reversal of Arkady's definition of nihilism, he would, in effect, "approach everything from a *non*-critical point of view." Leveraging his own exotic ethnicity, Misha wins the esteem of his friends by playing on their sympathies as fellow global pluralists: "Whenever the wisdom of having a sleepy Russian Gargantua clattering around the already tight quarters came up, I merely had to say something like 'Malevich!' or 'Tarkovksy!,'[38] letting the reflected sheen of my countrymen's accomplishments glisten off my Multicultural Studies medals."[39]

Though the novel seems to encourage us to accept the genuineness of Misha's passion for Rouenna as an individual—"This is a book about love"[40]—his attraction to her is also clearly bound up in his comic fetishizing of American ethnic diversity: he calls her his "giant multicultural swallow,"[41] for she is "Half Puerto Rican. And half German. And half Mexican and Irish and everything else besides."[42] In claiming Rouenna, he would dramatically reject his father's conservative Judaism, for she is, like Morgan in *The Russian Debutante's Handbook,* a figuration of the alluring but taboo shiksa (Yiddish: "non-Jewish woman"; Hebrew *shekets*: "impure," "loathsome thing"). Having been disfigured during a circumcision undertaken as an adult at his father's insistence, Misha finds a kind of secular, cosmopolitan redemption in Rouenna's sexual ministrations:

> She turned [his penis] over, found the most hideous spot on its underbelly—a vivid evocation of the bombing of Dresden—and, for the next 389 seconds (a handy clock helped me count), imparted on it a single, silent kiss.
> . . .
> I floated above the city [New York], glancing generously in each direction. The careless hooks and crags of Queens and Brooklyn, slivers of industry, quadrangles of brown-bricked terraced flats; the fanatic middle-class hopes of already half-darkened New Jersey tendering their resignation for the night; the carpeted grid of Manhattan sinking into the flat horizon, the garlands of yellow light—sharp, overreaching—that form the facades of skyscrapers, the garlands of yellow light—diffuse, flickering—that form the sprawl of tenements, the garlands of yellow light—swerving, opportunistic—that form the headlights of taxi caravans: the garlands of yellow light, aye, in their horizontal and vertical arrangements that form a final resting place for the collected hopes of our civilization.
>
> And to my father, I say: *I'm sorry, but this floating feeling, this yellow city at my feet, those full lips around what's left of me, this is my happiness, Papa. This is my pierogi.*[43]

Brought to mind here is Philip Roth's Portnoy, whose anxious process of assimilation also involves an erotic absorption of multitudes: he has been attempting to "discover America" by sleeping with multiple gentile women, he tells us, as "though my manifest destiny is to seduce a girl from each of the forty-eight states."[44] Misha seemingly will confirm to himself his own national and masculinist bona fides by seducing a symbol of the American melting pot.

After beginning an affair with Misha's rival Shteynfarb, however, Rouenna turns multiculturalist rhetoric—filtered through her professor's self-serving deployment of postcolonial theory and her own half-understanding—back on him:

> *[Shteynfarb says] you always viewed me from the Position of a Colonialist Oppresor. You always secretly look down at me. I tried to talk to you so many times about my Writing when I was in russia but you never seemed to listen. Its always you you you. Your ignoring me just like my family and thats going to hurt my self as-steam. Also Professor Shteynfarb says its wrong when you throw your shoe at your servant (I'm sorry, but I think thats true). Also he says its wrong when you an your friend alosha try to do your rapping and pretend your from the ghetto because thats also being a Colonialist. He gave me a book by Edward Said, which is super hard, but its worth it.*[45]

The satirical thrusts here target Shteynfarb's cynical manipulation of class and ethnic resentments, Rouenna's clumsy appeal to an emancipatory politics for the airing of private grievances, and Misha's complicity in cultural appropriations and abuses of power that contradict his professed ideals. Those ideals can function, Shteynfarb has implied, as a sort of enormous, self-serving buffet from which anyone might feed personal ambitions.

Some of the most lively skewering of multiculturalism's "omnivoracity" comes via Misha's fondness for the aggressive posturing of American hip-hop, a musical genre rooted in African American culture but, in the age of late capitalism, freely appropriated around the globe. Misha, who has taken on the alias Snack Daddy,[46] frequently launches into lyrics notable for their misogyny and crude stereotyping:

> *My name is Vainberg*
> *I like ho's*
> *Sniff 'em out*
> *Wid my Hebrew nose*
>
> *Pump that shit*
> *From 'round the back*
> *Big-booty ho*
> *Ack ack ack*[47]

Russia's own undiscriminating consumption is underscored in the receptivity of Lyuba, Misha's stepmother, to even cruder lyrics:

She stood up on the bed, and with her hands making jabbing urban motions, her hips thrusting like those of a fertile American university student, Lyuba sang:

Seexty-inch plasma screen
Bitch, you never seen
Such mad expensive shit
Poot my fingers on your clit
Uh, sex in the Lex
Check my dzhenuine Rolex
Vaiping cum off your tits
I'm busting phat beats
Right past yo' shoulder
It's over
Now go cook for my kids

"That's very pretty," I said. "Your English is improving."[48]

Lyuba's comically earnest and accented mimicry of a foreign cultural product—even the gender here is incongruous—satirizes not just the crudeness of the hip-hop genre and the *poshlost* of Russians who consume it, but Misha's own pretentious connoisseurship of African American exotica; his sophisticated "oeuvre," he tells us, "stretches from the old-school jams of Ice Cube, Ice-T, and Public Enemy to the sensuous contemporary rhythms of ghetto tech, a hybrid of Miami bass, Chicago ghetto tracks, and Detroit electronica. The modern reader may be familiar with 'Ass-N-Titties' by DJ Assault, perhaps the *seminal* work of the genre."[49] And, as a well-trained multiculturalist, he suspends all other judgments in his celebration of ostensibly authentic ethnic expression: "'In terms of popular music'—I spoke now with the authority of a former Multicultural Studies major—'you should listen mainly to East Coast hip-hop and ghetto tech from Detroit. We must reject European music categorically. Even so-called progressive house! Do you hear me, Lyuba?'"[50]

The vapidity of this manner of liberal politics, its practical equivalence to a self-indulgent escape from moral subtlety or responsibility in the pleasures of undiscriminating consumption, is made particularly clear in Shteyngart's descriptions of his protagonist's erotic life. Misha notes, for instance, his disappointment after an encounter with two Asian women—"They smelled, in a perfectly Russian manner, of dill and sweat. Some multiculturalism! Even our Asians are Russian"[51]—and his displeasure at being refused by a prostitute who objects to his national origin: "I like to think of the Hyatt as a multicultural space. And then some whore calls me a dirty Russian. Where's the respect?"[52]

He fulfills his name-fate as a gigantic mound of vanity in his consumption of pornography that he characteristically describes as well-intentioned voyeurism: "I watched all kinds of unfortunate women being degraded and humiliated, tied up, spat upon, forced to swallow gigantic penises, and I wished I could wipe off their dripping faces, whisk them away to some Minneapolis or Toronto, and teach them to take pleasure in a simple linear life far from their big-dicked tormentors."[53] Misha's compassionate impulses ultimately prove sterile, for his idealism tends to decline quickly into fatalism and self-indulgence:

> I asked myself, If I were to give each of them [a group of impoverished Russian children] US$100,000, would their lives change? Would they learn to become human beings upon completing their adolescence? Would the virus of our history be kept at bay by a cocktail of dollar-denominated humanism? Would they become, in a sense, Misha's Children? But even with my largesse, I could see nothing positive befalling them. A temporary respite from alcoholism, harlotry, heart disease, and depression. Misha's Children? Forget it. It would make more sense to have sex with their teacher and then buy her a refrigerator.[54]

Whatever guilt does remain with the protagonist is bought off during expensive telephone sessions with his psychotherapist, who apparently is himself something of a multicultural sophisticate: "I imagined Dr. Levine—his Semitic face freshly tanned from the beaches of Ipanema, his belly perfectly rounded from a judicious intake of *churrasco* and black beans—looking over the empty leather couch before him, the speakerphone turned on, the room ablaze with photographs of colorful Sioux tepees, perhaps suggesting the pathway to a better self, that tight little wigwam inside my heart."[55] The multicultural "Other" becomes here a sort of showpiece attesting to one's broadmindedness and refined tastes, as well as a confirmation of one's cultural power. Steven S. Lee, in applying the Slovenian philosopher Slavov Žižek's critique of identity politics to *Absurdistan,* noted the perverse logic at play: "Žižek writes that multiculturalism favors the elites of global capitalism—free from the confines of any single culture and condescending to those who are so confined. That is, these elites assert their superiority by claiming to respect multiple cultures. The result is the maintenance of a patronizing, upper- and upper-middle-class Eurocentrism, however concealed. . . . In short, Misha exemplifies Žižek's free-floating global elite, asserting progressive superiority through a fetish for rap music and brown women."[56]

Stranded in Absurdsvanï, Misha ultimately offers to become the nation's "Minister of Multicultural Affairs"[57] after explaining to the new government what multiculturalism involves. His ambitions for the role, which travesty the naive fantasies of inclusiveness that he absorbed at Accidental College, finally amount to little more than a vigorously sentimental affirmation of difference. The complexities of national politics will resolve themselves, according to Misha's vision, into an idyllic version of campus life at an American liberal arts college: "I would be in charge of minority relations. I would unite all the different people living in Absurdsvanï. And together we would hold festivals and conferences almost every day. We'd celebrate our identities. It would look very good in the eyes of the world. *I would be a uniter.*"[58] The italicized type of the final sentence seems to echo President George W. Bush's famous assertion that he was "a uniter, not a divider,"[59] and thus ironically links Misha's role with that of an assumed political opposite. As Misha will discover, his well-meaning efforts to bring multicultural harmony to at least one corner of the world are in fact being co-opted by cynical opportunists on the political right and the corporations with whom they are collaborating; Halliburton, the oil-field services company formerly led by the American vice president Dick Cheney, is repeatedly invoked. The civil war that traps Misha has been orchestrated, he discovers, by the new government itself, which sees value in setting the nation's ethnic factions against each other. As one official puts it, to "outsiders, it looks like a real war. Like we're tearing each other apart. Help, help, U.S.A. Save our oil."[60] Joseph Heller, whose character Milo Minderbinder in *Catch-22* bombs his own military in order to further his capitalist interests, is invoked here as corporations try to arrange at least the simulation of an emerging genocide in order to clear the way for more profiteering.[61] "Multiculturalism" functions in this milieu as a pretext for manipulating international attention, which can then be used to lure aid and investment dollars, as well as kickbacks for well-placed individuals.

The reduction of cultural identities to mere commodities is explored further in Shteyngart's withering indictment of the superficiality and partiality of American sympathies. As Misha explains to an Absurdsvanï oligarch, American respect for ethnicity is fundamentally entangled with the pleasures of media-driven consumption, and, without the promise of those pleasures, any particular ethnic "product" will have trouble becoming visible: "no one knows where your country is or who you are. You don't have a familiar ethnic cuisine; your diaspora, from what I understand, is mostly in Southern California, three time zones removed from the national media in New York; and you don't have a recognizable, long-simmering conflict like the one between the Israelis and the Palestinians, where people in the richer nations can take sides and argue over the dinner table."[62] The limits of America's ethnic sympathies are further explicated by an Israeli agent who reports that, in focus groups testing knowledge of foreign peoples, the American public failed miserably at recognizing the Absurdsvanïs:

> "The Congolese are clearly black, so that strikes a chord with all the respondents. Like them or not, you got plenty of blacks in America. The Indonesians have funny eyes, so they're Asian. Probably work hard and raise dutiful children. Good for them. Then you get the Absurdis. They're sort of dark, but not really black. They look a little Indonesian, but they've got round eyes. Are they Arabs? Italians? Persians? We finally settle on 'taller Mexicans,' which is another way of saying we're fucked.
>
> "Then we really let the cat out of the bag. We tell them, 'Look, there's a genocide happening, and the U.S. can invade one of the following ten countries.' We give them a list of countries, real and imaginary. We've got Djibouti, Yolanda, Costa Rica, Eastern Tuchusland, Absurdsvanï, and so forth. Guess what came in dead last, even behind the reviled Homoslavia? That's right. See, the way 'Absurdsvanï' is pronounced and spelled, it's utterly impossible for an American to feel anything for it. You have to be able to use a country as a child's first name to get anywhere. *Rwanda* Jones. *Somalia* Cohen. *Timor* Jackson. *Bosnia* Lewis-Wright. And then you got this *Republika Absurdsvanï*. Hopeless."[63]

Misha is of course quite willing to play the ethnic marketing game himself in his official ministerial role. A long set piece that seems somewhat awkwardly thrust into the narrative presents Misha's irreverent major initiative as the Minister of Multicultural Affairs: the construction of an Absurdsvanï Holocaust museum. His outlandish grant application is presented, with a nod to Jonathan Swift, in a chapter titled "A Modest Proposal." Such a museum, claims Misha, will help catalyze American and Israeli support for the nation and exploit the marketability of a well-connected ethnic group within the multicultural West. The challenge, he explains, is to overcome "the oversaturation of the Holocaust brand in media and academe."[64] With so many others vying to memorialize this singular event and mobilize support for Israel as well as for Jews around the world, it can be difficult to have one's voice heard.

The ironies here are exceptionally complex. Misha, as an idealistic multiculturalist, will seek to leverage respect for his own ethnic group, many of whose members he detests, on behalf of a cause he does not find compelling. Thus he may aid, in seeming defiance of multicultural fair play, one of the two warring ethnic groups in the region even though he finds that group corrupt and essentially indistinguishable from its rival. As he says during an imagined conversation with his father: "I want to believe in something, too, Papa, . . . [just] like you believed in Israel. I want to help the Sevo people. I'm not stupid. I know they're no good. But they're better than their neighbors."[65] Shteyngart has audaciously mocked here the ostensible sentimentality surrounding narratives of the Holocaust, its exploitation by Jews and gentiles alike for political and commercial benefit, and the seeming irrationality of all allegiances made along ethnic lines, which is a notable departure from Vladimir's appreciation of his grandmother's warning, in *The Russian Debutante's Handbook,* about the need for Jewish solidarity.

While multiculturalism is satirized for its fetishizing and commodifying of identity along with its inevitable separation of ethnic groups into agreeable winners and forgettable losers, *mono*culturalism—that is, a resolute commitment to the interests of a single religious or ethnic identity—is also singled out for ironic treatment. A longstanding source of violence in Absurdsvanï is the rivalry between the Svanï and the Sevo, who "started out as one people."[66] Although they are both Christian, they are viciously set against each other by their opposing views on the direction in which Christ's footrest should be slanted in representations of the Crucifixion. Devoted "true believers" defend a patently meaningless article of faith, ignoring the arbitrariness of their—and anyone else's—convictions. Shteyngart may well have had in mind here a specific historical event: after the ascendance of Moscow as the symbolic center of the Orthodox world in the seventeenth century, Patriarch Nikon undertook a series of hotly debated reforms, many of which concerned the liturgical representation of Christ. As Antone Minard explained,

> The new Slavonic spelling of the name "Jesus" made it closer to the traditional Greek pronunciation: instead of "Isus" it became "Iisus." But the changes caused tensions within the Russian community. Within the context of mythological consciousness, the change of the signifier led inevitably to the change of the signified: the "new" name of Jesus could not be received as the name of Christ, the object of faith. The wrong name could belong only to a wrong Christ, the Antichrist. Another novelty also concerned Christ: a newly adapted way of making the sign of the cross. Finally, new prescriptions for the order of processions in the liturgy were published: instead of going clockwise, "with the Sun" in Russian, they now had to go counterclockwise, "against the Sun." To go against the Sun meant, for many, to go against Christ the Sun of Justice. As processions were an important element in the sacraments and sacramental, the "wrong" processions made the sacraments "wrong," that is, not merely invalid but sacrilegious. All of these things instigated a schism in the Russian Church.[67]

The "Old Believers," who would not embrace the reforms, were "subjected to merciless persecution"[68] and eventually devised new ways of afflicting *themselves* in order to affirm their marginalized beliefs: "Avvakum, their leader, introduced a new element into their Christ-centered devotion: self-sacralization through sufferings and death, including suicide. Collective suicides by fire (about 20,000 by the end of the 17th century) demonstrated the popularity of his teaching."[69]

The senselessly destructive conflict between the Svanï and the Sevo also brings to mind an American literary precursor: the Shepherdsons and Grangerfords from Mark Twain's *Adventures of Huckleberry Finn,* proud families from the American South who have been assaulting each other for years but cannot quite remember why. These warring clans consider themselves devout and wash away at church any guilt that might have accumulated from their mutual attacks, while continually and dramatically failing to love their neighbors. Like Misha, Huck is personally endangered after getting caught in the middle of a deadly feud, which from his outsider's perspective—and with his instinct for avoiding conflict in order to preserve his personal freedom—seems pointlessly destructive:

> Next Sunday we all went to church, about three mile, everybody a-horseback. The men took their guns along, so did Buck, and kept them between their knees or stood them handy against the wall. The Shepherdsons done the same. It was pretty ornery preaching—all about brotherly love, and suchlike tiresomeness; but everybody said it was a good sermon, and they all talked it over going home, and had such a powerful lot to say about faith, and good works, and free grace, and preforeordestination, and I don't know what all, that it did seem to me to be one of the roughest Sundays I had run across yet.[70]

A more mature observer than Huck—though still a naive one—Misha struggles to frame his apprehension of outrageous religious hypocrisy within his pluralist ideals: "I believe that when confronted with the irrational, we must not laugh, even when laughter is richly deserved."[71]

Part of Shteyngart's satirical point here—which seems consonant with the so-called New Atheism, a movement begun around the time Shteyngart began publishing and led by such figures as Christopher Hitchens, Richard Dawkins, Daniel Dennett, and Sam Harris—is that all kinds of violence and depravity are made possible by religiosity. As Misha paraphrases the teachings of Jesus to Saint Sevo, "I want you to get your homeys together, get your pointiest utensils, and spear the bejesus out of all your enemies. And when you're through spearing, I want you to fuck every underage cutie in town."[72] The famous questions broached in Dostoevsky's *The Brothers Karamazov* concerning the relationship between faith and morality—"But what will become of men . . . without God and immortal life? All things are lawful then, they can do what they like?"[73]—are answered ironically by Shteyngart and the New Atheists, who suggest that it is in fact faith that sets competing factions against one another and licenses the most extreme sorts of aggression and perversity. Hitchens often quoted the Nobel physicist Stephen Weinberg in defense of this argument: "With or without religion, good people can behave well and bad people can do evil; but for good people to do evil—that takes religion."[74] Faith comes to seem, moreover, not just irrational and destructive but also a model instance of "false consciousness"; a ruling elite in Absurdsvanï shrewdly cultivates religious schisms, keeping the masses distracted and making possible various kinds of exploitation.

The novel's most complicated and provocative treatment of religious identity comes, however, in its representation of Jewish religious faith itself. As a "deeply secular Jew who finds no comfort in either nationalism or religion"[75] and who cherishes his superiority over "second-rate"[76] Jews (that is, those who practice a devout form of Judaism), Misha reacts against his father's declaration that he will always be limited in his identity, not a citizen of the world, or even a cosmopolitan New Yorker, but always simply a "Jew, Jew, Jew."[77] He finds ample grounds for animosity toward Orthodox Judaism after being brutally and incompetently circumcised by a group of Hasidic men, and his permanently deformed sexual organ—which has come to resemble a "crushed purple bug"[78]—makes numerous comic appearances throughout the novel.[79] Misha's multicultural intolerance is dramatically illustrated when, while traveling first-class on an Austrian Airlines flight, he is gravely offended by the presence of a Hasidic man who insists on being served kosher food:

> He was in his thirties, scraggly-bearded and pimpled, as are they all, with red eyes round as coins. He did not wear the usual top hat, just a jaunty fedora, beneath which peeked out the half-moon of his yarmulke. I doubted he had actually bought a first-class ticket, this citizen of the Eternal *Shtetl,* so perhaps some kind of upgrade scheme was in effect. You never know with these people. . . . Would it be eliminationist of me to say that I wanted to kill him? Are there certain feelings that, as a Jew, I may safely harbor in my fat heart that a non-Jew may not? Would it really be self-hatred to despise this man with whom I shared nothing more than a squirrelly strand of DNA?[80]

There is no place, it seems, for *this* man within Misha's multiculturalism, which has been replaced, temporarily, with something like its grotesque inversion.

What exactly is to be made of this scene? Many readers may find such material problematic—as Adrian Wanner has noted, "Shteyngart's fictional caricatures of Jews come dangerously close to anti-Semitic stereotypes and Jewish self-hatred"[81]—regardless of the obvious ironies here, which one assumes are meant to provoke an awareness of the uncanny absurdity of Misha's eruption.

Olga Gershenson and David Schneer's brief summary of the novel's representation of Hasidic Jews suggests that Shteyngart was exploring here the sizable "gaps in understanding" between globally dispersed Jewish populations and thus offering "reminders of internal Jewish diversity, of which now post-Soviet Jews are a part."[82] This explanation is certainly plausible, though it does not seem to account for the ferocity of Misha's attack on the Hasids; the airplane scene was not broached by Gershenson and Schneer. Perhaps Shteyngart's aim in showing us that ferocity was to expose self-hatred as the absorption of racial prejudices among Jews, especially those, like Misha, who have absorbed everything else in their search for belonging and fear being singled out as preferring and advocating some kind of cultural singularity in a pluralist world. Misha is of course acutely aware of Eastern European anti-Semitism, and he describes several instances of being assaulted for his racial otherness, although his great physical bulk, along with his great wealth, insulates him from any real damage. No matter how rapidly the post-Soviet republics may be shifting to a globalized sensibility, the persistence of old prejudices that enforce Jewish marginality means that Misha is always at risk of being identified as an interloper:

> "Excuse me," he said in Russian, the lingua franca of the former Soviet empire, "who are you by nationality?"
>
> I sadly held up my Russian passport. "No, no," [he] laughed. "I mean by *nationality.*"
>
> I saw what he was after. "Jew," I said, patting my nose.[83]

Another possibility is to see Misha's reaction as Shteyngart's critique of the typically hidden or disavowed intolerance lurking within pluralist sensibilities themselves—an unacknowledged but potent aversion to anything that looks like fundamentalism and might clash with the cosmopolitan values esteemed by so-called multiculturalists; that is, multicultural tolerance hits its endpoint here, itself becoming fanatical and irrational, when it confronts those who do not subscribe to its own pluralist values.[84]

Misha's knotty prejudices and compromised idealism provide ample and often light comic fodder in *Absurdistan,* but the novel consistently provides grim reminders—typically glimpsed beyond its narrator's mountainous narcissism—of the real suffering of the vulnerable. Consider, for instance, Misha's description of Lyuba, his stepmother, before they engage in intercourse: "Lyuba had a lean, athletic body (especially for someone who did nothing all day), interrupted only by a swatch of shiny, hardened skin running along one hip and dipping toward her genitals, where a relative had set fire to her when she was twelve."[85] Or this scene, when he is holed up in an Absurdsvanï hotel under siege during the civil war: "Lefèvre, upon seeing my bulk spilling over the tiny Soviet bed so that each leg and arm hung suspended like a ham at a Castilian tapas bar, started laughing with every atom of his marinated red face. But the joke was on him several days later, when he committed suicide in our bathroom."[86] Misha's witnessing of a mass execution of innocents spurs his clumsy political activities in Absurdsvanï, but he is strikingly unable to respond to injustice and misery appropriately: in a telling illustration of this failure, he punches a woman in the face and then flees after she offers to prostitute her five-year-old daughter.[87] Multiculturalism's celebration of the world's diversity tends, Shteyngart has implied, to deny, or at least shy from acknowledging, the inveteracy of human frailty and cruelty, the reality of evil. In other words, in its uncritical receptivity to cultural differences, it undermines moral efforts that seem to demand discriminating, focused condemnation.

Misha himself ends up in a monocultural refuge at last, something like a mirror image of Vladimir Girshkin's Cleveland in *The Russian Debutante's Handbook*, where he is sheltered by a group of devout "Mountain Jews" amid the turmoil of the Absurdsvanï civil war. These Jews are fans of his father, Boris Vainberg, who strikes them as an apparently compelling example of Jewish endurance and capitalist success. They have even erected a plaque in his honor, on which his guiding motto—made famous by Malcolm X in the context of the African American civil rights movement—has been reproduced: "BY ANY MEANS NECESSARY."[88] Recall the deployment of the phrase by Vladimir's grandmother in Shteyngart's first novel, and its largely unironic status there as a kind of ethical touchstone for Jewish survival. Vladimir is, as it were, taken out of himself by his contemplation of the phrase, jarred from his Russian fantasies of ethnic crossing and escape by a reminder of his involuntary identification with a persecuted group. Misha's use of the phrase seems to drain it of both its communal dimension and its ethical seriousness, as he declares his intention to abandon his romantic affair with Nana Nanabragovna, a member of one of Absurdsvanï's ethnic factions, and make another attempt, using all the privileges his wealth provides, to return to Rouenna in New York. As he tells his manservant, "I don't want her [Nana]. And I don't want her people. . . . We're going to New York. By any means necessary."[89] Dean J. Franco astutely pointed out that Boris and Misha's use of the famous phrase differs from Malcolm X's, since the latter was interested in a political program for securing group rights whereas "Misha's adoption of [the motto] signals his self-conscious pivot away from a superficial devotion to multiculturalism and toward a stripped-down, brutal ethos of self-interest."[90] That self-interest continues to involve a connoisseurship of multicultural America, for the novel concludes with Misha's sentimental fantasy of life with Rouenna in a "grand and decrepit"[91] residence near subsidized housing in the Bronx:

> The old men playing dominoes for money; five-year-old Bebo, Franky, Marelyn, and Aysha kicking around a dusty football; their older cousins skipping the world's most artful double Dutch; teenage moms and dads talking sex at each other across the stoops, calling their little ones *tiguerito*, "little gangster"; the sneakers hanging off the telephone poles; the tricked-out Mitsubishi Monteros pumping salsa across the streets; the moms reading the coupon pages like newspapers; the stores with no name but PLAY LOTTERY HERE; the roses sticking out of the iron grilles of housing-project windows.[92]

What disappears here for Misha is the pretense of contributing to a common good—the ostensible essence of his liberal idealism—leaving only a satisfying retreat to a cosmopolitan milieu which can maintain a pleasurable cinematic status for him, since he will not himself have to read coupon pages in order to consume New York's sensuous offerings. In this darkly comic finale, "by any means necessary" amounts to a kind of cowardly retreat from judgment—which is perhaps the culmination of Zygmunt Bauman's definition of multiculturalism—and a hardened turn to self-preservation.

CHAPTER 4

Super Sad True Love Story

The publication of *Super Sad True Love Story* in 2010 was a major literary event. The novel's marketing campaign included an initial YouTube book trailer starring the Hollywood actor James Franco (who had been enrolled in a creative writing course at Columbia University taught by Shteyngart) and, for the softcover edition, a follow-up that featured Paul Giamatti.[1] In these short videos Shteyngart comically played "himself" as a buffoonish, illiterate, barely assimilated immigrant, though the novel itself is much less manic and farcical than *The Russian Debutante's Handbook* or *Absurdistan* in its explorations of ethnic identity.

Super Sad True Love Story presents a near-future dystopia as the United States collapses into financial—and, seemingly, moral—bankruptcy. Owing massive debts to China and other creditors, the nation is, as the novel opens, on the verge of being taken over and parceled up by various foreign states and corporations, the distinction having been largely eroded. A totalitarian social order now thoroughly monitors and manipulates the lives of citizens, most of whom remain preoccupied, via a kind of super-smartphone called an "äppärät," with inane entertainment and material acquisition. This culture should be largely familiar to us: it is the consumerist and technology-obsessed America of the early twenty-first century, only more so.

The novel's central protagonist, another Russian Jewish American in search of love and belonging, is Lenny Abramov, a thirty-nine-year-old salesman in "the Post-Human Services division"[2] of a corporation hawking technologies that promise eternal life. His sense of isolation comes not from his ethnic identity, but rather from a lingering allegiance to an earlier, predigital era and from his fear that, because he is no longer young, he has little to offer others in a youth-obsessed world. Though rather timid and ineffectual, Lenny—an ironic "Leonard," from Old High German *Leonhard,* "lion-hearted"[3]—has, he tells us, recently committed himself to scientific rejuvenation and finally immortality. He begins the narrative by reflecting on Whitney Houston's pop song "The Greatest Love of All," dismissing its recommendation that adults relinquish "selfhood in favor of future generations," since, by his reckoning, "children are our future only in the most narrow, transitive sense."[4] This ironic Abraham will not be commanded to sacrifice his child but will instead choose to abandon a commitment to any offspring in favor of endless self-preservation. In fact he will aspire to his name-fate: the biblical Abram, who becomes Abraham, combines in his name the Hebrew *ab* ("father") and *ram* ("raise, exalt," especially reflexively, "raise or exalt *oneself*").[5] Lenny would become a father, that is, not to an entire people, but to his own exalted self: "I just have to be good and I have to believe in myself. I just have to stay off the trans fats and the hooch. I just have to drink plenty of green tea and alkanized water and submit my genome to the right people. I will need to re-grow my melting liver, replace the entire circulatory system with 'smart blood,' and find someplace safe and warm (but not too warm) to while away the angry seasons and the holocausts."[6] Lenny's ambition is prompted by his encounter with a twenty-four-year-old Korean American named Eunice (Greek: "good/well-achieved victory"[7]) Park (a name perhaps suggestive of the anthropomorphic remains of "Nature"), in whom he locates a youthful, pastoral raison d'être amid the nation's Gothicized endtimes.[8] Their doomed affair forms the "super sad true love story" of the title, the phrasing itself mimicking the routine hyperbole and linguistic degradation that define this commercially saturated, relentlessly *poshlost* world.

Though it departs from Shteyngart's first two novels in its incorporation of elements from the science-fiction genre, *Super Sad True Love Story* in fact takes up and extends a number of themes broached in those works. In *The Russian Debutante's Handbook,* Vladimir Girshkin notes the contemporary decline of literacy in "post-Reagan/Bush Manhattan with its youth pierced, restless, weaned on flashing image and verbally disinclined"[9] and contrasts the artificiality and sterility of American life with the sensuous qualities of his Soviet youth: the perspiration of his American girlfriend Francesca is, he claims, "not the gamy Russian sweat [he] remembered from his childhood, [but] rather American sweat, sweat denatured by deodorant, sweat that smelled purely metallic, like blood."[10] The ahistorical and spiritually antiseptic characteristics of contemporary America are central to *Super Sad,* which focuses much of its satire on the ascendance of a toxically superficial, thoroughly denatured and "virtualized" youth culture. *Absurdistan*'s representation of the destabilizing effects of late capitalism, and the cruelties associated with extreme polarities in wealth distribution, finds new expression here too, as America itself is overwhelmed and violently refashioned by the forces of globalization. Moreover, the earlier novel's indictment of contemporary multiculturalism as a form of amoral consumerism—a reduction of the world to, as Zygmunt Bauman put it, "a gigantic department store"[11]—is hyperbolized in Shteyngart's representation of a culture that would commodify, and ultimately cheapen, every human interaction.

Lenny reads Chekhov and wonders at his parents' Soviet past, but, in contrast to what happened with Vladimir Girshkin and Misha Vainberg, his negotiation of Russianness is given relatively little play in the novel. As he tells us, "I have never been to Russia. I have not had the chance to love it and hate it the way my parents have. I have my own dying empire to contend with, and I do not wish for any other."[12] The narrative's exploration of Jewish identity is more prominent, for Shteyngart created a conspicuous symbolic structure by giving names from the Hebrew Bible to important characters—Abramov (Abraham), Joshua, David, and Noah—and by setting Post-Human Services in a former synagogue, where "the outline of the Ten Commandments" and "the words 'You Shall Have No Other Gods Before Me' [are] still stenciled into the window in English and Hebrew."[13] In a scene at the Bronx Zoo where he observes an elephant, Lenny's secular Jewishness, and its embodiment in his own rather long nose, is linked to his desire to raise himself beyond mortality: "The elephant knows there is nothing after this life and very little in it. The elephant is aware of his eventual extinction and he is hurt by it, reduced by it, made to feel his solitary nature, he who will eventually trample his way through bush and scrub to lie down and die where his mother once trembled at her haunches to give him life. Mother, aloneness, entrapment, extinction. The elephant is essentially an Ashkenazi animal, but a wholly rational one—it too wants to live forever."[14] Jews are waggishly posited in the novel as the ultimate American insiders: a villainous secretary of defence named Rubenstein (Hebrew *reuben,* "Behold, a son!") rules the nation through a puppet president, and an equally villainous man named Joshua "Joshie" Goldman spearheads the scientific quest for immortality.[15] Joshie seems a sort of ironic Joshua leading his people to the promised land (amid genocidal slaughter) and an even more ironic Jesus, selling eternal life to the faithful: "Joshua" and "Jesus" both come to English from the Hebrew name "Yehoshua," or "saved of God." Lenny sees Joshie as a paternal figure, and stakes out a plan in his diary to win his esteem and protection through a shared sense of ethnic vulnerability: "Evoke father-like bond in response to political situation. Talk about what happened on the plane [during the return voyage to America]; evoke Jewish feelings of terror and injustice."[16] When Lenny and Eunice visit Joshie at his apartment, Lenny effectively identifies his boss with the Savior after being struck by how young he looks after his regime of anti-aging treatments: "I was looking at dechronification in action. I was looking at Joshie Goldman himself, his body reverse-engineered into a thick young mass of tendons and forward motion. 'Jesus Christ,' I said."[17]

In spite of the ironies noted above, *Super Sad True Love Story* seems much less cynical than Shteyngart's previous novels in its representation of the *value* of ethnic and religious traditions as a means of orienting oneself in a cosmopolitan age. Eunice's Korean heritage is lampooned as both psychologically damaging and ridiculously compromised in its Western transplantation, but by the novel's end she nevertheless seems to discover within it a vital antidote, however qualified and tenuous, to the depthless immediacy and selfishness of contemporary life. Whereas Lenny's Russian and Jewish roots offer him little in the way of guidance during "the Rupture"—this novel's sardonic version of the Rapture and Second Coming, during which Joshie attempts to clear a path to eternal life for wealthy souls like himself—Eunice finds genuine purpose and comfort in turning to, and acting in accordance with, what she takes to be a Christian imperative to love and aid her neighbor. In representing Eunice's transformation, and indeed in exploring the "love story" at the heart of this narrative, Shteyngart adopted a much more earnest tone than in his previous works—perhaps suggesting his intent to move beyond a predominantly satirical mode and locate, against a *backdrop* that remains farcical, besieged but enduring possibilities for individual redemption.

Super Sad True Love Story has enjoyed a robust commercial and critical success. It won the Bollinger Everyman Wodehouse Prize and the Salon Book Award for fiction, while also being cited by a number of publications as one of the best novels of the year. Michael Wood's review praised the author's stylistic mastery: "The sheer exhilaration of the writing in this book—Lenny's confessional tones, Eunice's teenage slang—is itself a sort of answer to the flattened-out horrors of the world it depicts."[18] Michiko Kakutani reiterated familiar claims about Shteyngart's successful amalgamation of Russian and American literary, or, in her example, cinematic, traditions: the novel "reflects [Shteyngart's] dual heritage, combining the dark soulfulness of Russian literature with the antic inventiveness of postmodern American writing; the tenderness of the Chekhovian tradition with the hormonal high jinks of a Judd Apatow movie."[19] Aaron Thier, writing in the *Nation,* expressed some reservations, however, about Shteyngart's turn toward a supposedly stripped-down and conservative mode:

> What will be striking to anyone familiar with Shteyngart's writing is the sobriety with which he approaches the subjects of love and mortality [in *Super Sad True Love Story*]. What will also be striking is the degree to

> which he has abandoned many of the tonal and structural features that distinguished his first two novels. The writing here is utilitarian rather than exuberant; story is more important than scene; the men are not always fools and the women are not always beautiful cartoons. It is an altogether more conventional book, which is not necessarily good or bad, but it means that it's the kind of book Shteyngart might previously have held in contempt.[20]

One remarkable feature of the novel's critical reception so far—and a testament to the broad cultural relevance of Shteyngart's satire—is the way it has been cited by commentators working within a stunningly wide range of disciplines. Annie McClanahan, who investigated the "relationship between personhood and credit . . . [across] the history of credit under capitalism" in an essay published in *Representations,* affirmed that *Super Sad True Love Story* "shows us how the credit score, the social person, and literary character remain entangled."[21] Writing in the *Journal of Aging Studies,* Ulla Kriebernegg contended that the novel "subversively deconstructs normative age concepts and challenges the binary opposition of 'young' and 'old' by [caricaturing its] characters' obsession with youth and beauty and their stereotypical assumptions regarding aging and old age."[22] An anonymous author in the *Economist* complimented the novel's accurate representation of the United States' precarious financial status: "America presents a 'grave risk to the international system of corporate governance and exchange mechanisms,' says a Chinese central banker after a trip to New York. That is from the novel. The 'international currency system is the product of the past,' says China's president before a trip to Washington, D.C. That is from real life."[23] Carolyn Marvin, in an essay published in *Mobile Media & Communication* that explores the ways in which new communications technologies have affected social interactions, pointed to the novel as exemplary of critical new phenomena: "By ranking digital influence and participation, new aggregators of legibility . . . create novel measures of social worth, performative obligations, and formats for surveillance (comically and chillingly elaborated in [*Super Sad True Love Story*])."[24] A recent article in the journal *Transcultural Psychiatry,* which surveys some of the ways in which social-networking culture can "simplify and flatten relationships and intimacy," suggests that the novel "depicts the nadir of this flattening of social life . . . in which the events of everyday life, including romantic encounters, are blogged and rated online in real-time and achieving high ratings counts for more than the quality of the human encounter."[25]

Shteyngart set his love story within a suggestively Orwellian state marked by sprawling surveillance, a bullying police presence, and a systematic corruption of language that seems to inhibit clear and independent thinking: "It's *1984*, baby,"[26] as one American ex-patriate miserably remarks. The novel's socio-political backdrop seems at least as indebted, however, to more colorful dystopias, such as—to cite just two obvious examples—Aldous Huxley's novel *Brave New World* and Terry Gilliam's film *Brazil*. Totalitarianism in *Super Sad True Love Story* has its gray, brutalist dimensions, but it is more characteristically garish in appearance, its coercive power exerted through carefully engineered, hedonistic enticements. On his return to New York from an extended business trip in Italy, Lenny encounters the American Restoration Authority (or ARA, the novel's version of the Department of Homeland Security), which has recently claimed additional supervisory powers. His primary interlocutor here is an ingratiating cartoon otter, which asks him to reveal, among other more prosaic information, his financial status and the details of his sexual life overseas:

> An electronic version of John Cougar Mellencamp's "Pink Houses" ("Ain't that America, somethin' to see, baby!") twanged in my ear, and then a pixilated version of the plucky otter shuffled onto my äppärät screen, carrying on his back the letters ARA, which dissolved into the shimmering legend: American Restoration Authority.
>
> The otter stood up on his hind legs, and made a show of dusting himself off. "Hi there pa'dner!" he said, his electronic voice dripping with adorable carnivalesque. "My name is Jeffrey Otter and I *bet* we're going to be friends!"
>
> . . .
>
> "You know Americans get lonely abroad. Happens all the time! That's why I never leave the brook where I was born. What's the point? Tell me, for statistical purposes, did you have any intimate physical relationships with any *non*-Americans during your stay?"[27]

In its more aggressive communications, the ARA expressly prohibits cognition, while characteristically adding a fig leaf of civic boosterism: "IT IS FORBIDDEN TO ACKNOWLEDGE THE EXISTENCE OF THIS VEHICLE ('THE OBJECT') UNTIL YOU ARE .5 MILES FROM THE SECURITY PERIMETER OF JOHN F. KENNEDY INTERNATIONAL AIRPORT. BY READING THIS SIGN YOU HAVE DENIED EXISTENCE OF THE OBJECT AND IMPLIED CONSENT . . .—AMERICAN RESTORATION AUTHORITY . . . 'TOGETHER WE'LL SURPRISE THE WORLD!'"[28] These communications imply a markedly sinister form of *poshlost*, for totalitarian surveillance and disciplinary control are disguised, if barely, within affectedly innocuous appeals for cooperation. Until his eventual return to Italy, Lenny endures a series of harassing encounters with various digital representatives of the state, who remain suspicious about his status as an American, an ironic allusion, perhaps, to the fate of Shteygnart's protagonists in his previous novels.

Milan Kundera's *The Unbearable Lightness of Being* (1984), another love story set against the rise of an authoritarian regime, in this case the actual Soviet takeover of Czechoslovakia in the late 1960s, forms an important intertext here. Kundera's novel charts, among other horrors, new and frightening violations of privacy:

> Jan Prochazka, a forty-year-old Czech novelist with the strength and vitality of an ox, began criticizing public affairs vociferously even before 1968. He then became one of the best-loved figures of the Prague Spring, that dizzying liberalization of Communism which ended with the Russian invasion. Shortly after the invasion the press initiated a smear campaign against him, but the more they smeared, the more people liked him. Then (in 1970, to be exact), the Czech radio broadcast a series of private talks between Prochazka and a professor friend of his which had taken place years before (that is, in the spring of 1968). For a long time, neither of them had any idea that the professor's flat was bugged and their every step dogged. Prochazka loved to regale his friends with hyperbole and excess. Now his excesses had become a weekly radio series.[29]

Like Shteyngart, Kundera has explored the way all citizens are conscripted into the role of apparatchik ("Communist spy or agent") and all private experience is offered up as public entertainment: Tereza "told Tomas that morning about how her mother had read her secret diary at the dinner table to an accompaniment of guffaws. When a private talk over a bottle of wine is broadcast on the radio, what can it mean but that the world is turning into a concentration camp?"[30] Both authors are concerned too with the soullessness of life within the apparat, the ultimate emptiness of being elevated—as in Lenny's name-fate as an *Ab-ram,* a "father," "exalted (above others)" or "self-exalted"—on its meretricious stages: "But many also died without being directly subjected to persecution; the hopelessness pervading the entire country penetrated the soul to the body, shattering the latter. Some ran desperately from the favor of a regime that wanted to endow them with the honor of displaying them side by side with its new leaders."[31] Lenny praises Kundera's novel and reads sections of it to Eunice, with mixed success: "On page eight, I read a part I had underlined as a moody, unlaid teenager. 'What happens but once . . . might as well not have happened at all. If we have only one life to live, we might as well have not lived at all.' . . . I re-read the lines again, slowly, with emphasis, directly into Eunice's pert, wax-free ear, and as I did so I wondered if perhaps it was this book that had launched my search for immortality."[32] Eunice is intrigued by Kundera's work initially but finally just confused, largely because she is less interested than Lenny in the eternal and much more at home in a social order in which what used to be called "private life" has either been voluntarily surrendered or smoothly seized by technocrats. Very little that happens in this world escapes at least potential observation by strangers, and even the text before us—in the form of Lenny's diary entries and Eunice's emails—has been stolen, as is made known at the novel's end, by hackers who have made it available in its current commodified form.

The *poshlost* world satirized in Shteyngart's fiction has much in common, moreover, with what Kundera's work critiques as kitsch: that is, "the mask of beauty [the Communist world] tried to wear,"[33] which amounts to "a folding screen set up to curtain off death."[34] Both authors are concerned with the falseness that seems essential to the functioning of tyrannical regimes and with the lethality lurking beyond it. Much more powerful stagecraft is available, of course, to Shteyngart's neo-totalitarian dramatists, who can effortlessly bewitch audiences with pleasurable spectacles, whereas Kundera's citizens still have enough relative independence, for the most part, *not* to suspend their disbelief. Though the oppressive political order in *Super Sad True Love Story* is in some ways similar to Kundera's Sovietized Czechoslovakia, it has seamlessly merged with a hyperbolic form of American-style capitalism: military checkpoints and the bullying of shadowy agents coexist with, and in fact reinforce, citizens' indulgence in ostentatious hedonism, outrageous self-expression, and relentless consumerism. The "GlobalTeens" social network—something like Facebook, though even more comprehensive and intrusive as an interface with the world—produces its own supervisory discipline by manipulating its users with subtle or not-so-subtle forms of shaming and by bathing communication in a kind of linguistic solvent: "GLOBALTEENS SUPER HINT: *Harvard Fashion School studies show excessive typing makes wrists large and unattractive. Be a GlobalTeen forever—switch to Images today!*"[35]

In his essay "Moscow," first published in 1927, Walter Benjamin presciently reflected on the end of privacy enacted by Bolshevism: "The bureaucracy, political activity, the press are so powerful that no time remains for interests that do not converge with them. Nor any space. Apartments that earlier accommodated single families in their five to eight rooms now often lodge eight. Through the hall door, one steps into a little town. More often still, into an army camp."[36] In Shteyngart's version of the United States, Soviet and American worlds have merged, and one continually steps through the portals of various technologies into an enormous militarized "town," where all space is effectively common. With private life largely emptied out into public spaces, nearly everything one does is subject to social appraisal and regulation: "credit poles" reveal one's financial status to the world as one walks by them, ubiquitous digital prosthetics collect and "stream" every formerly intimate detail of one's formerly personal history, and even transparent clothing, which has become fashionable among women, denudes one before one's peers.

At Lenny's workplace, tyrannical scrutiny reaches beneath the skin as enormous boards continuously update the chemical coordinates of employees: "[They displayed] the results of our latest physicals, our methylation and homocysteine levels, our testosterone and estrogen, our fasting insulin and triglycerides, and, most important, our 'mood + stress indicators,' which were always supposed to read 'positive/playful/ready to contribute' but which, with enough input from competitive co-workers, could be changed to 'one moody betch today' or 'not a team playa this month.'"[37] These boards have been repurposed from Italian railroad stations, in what is perhaps an allusion to the fascist Mussolini, who made sure, according to popular legend, that his nation's trains always ran on time. Humans—their inner machinery exposed before their peers—will run on time too or be discarded for breaking down. Away from work, Lenny uses "RateMe Plus technology"[38]—a seeming pun on "Rape Me" and thus suggestive of the sort of voluntary invasion of privacy at issue here—in order to share his romantic estimations of others and to know others' estimations of him. In a humiliating episode at a bar, he "FACs"—that is, "forms a community"—with other customers, briefly making contact with a group of strangers and ostensibly sharing intimate information ranging from his economic status, history of familial abuse, and sexual preferences, which are ranked by favorite orifice. The community thus formed is temporary, cynical, and caustically uncivil, the information shared within it temporary and exceedingly superficial, but it provides an essential means in this culture of knowing others and oneself. State and commercial powers mediate this comprehensive visibility and are thus able to expand disciplinary control within the routines of individual self-expression and pleasure seeking.[39]

The name given to the central technology satirized in the novel—the äppärät—cleverly suggests a blending of the communist and capitalist. The English word "apparat," which comes to us from the Latin *appărātus* (a "preparation" or "getting ready" of things, including the "instruments" that one might use to make an ostentatious display), refers to "The party machine of the Communist party in Russia, etc." An "apparatchik," moreover, is one who belongs to the party machine—or, more darkly, a Communist agent or spy. In Shteyngart's dystopia, citizens are leashed to their äppäräti, which they use to shop, entertain themselves, and manage their public standing. This profound networking of citizens makes it easy, needless to say, for state and commercial powers to track and influence their behavior in ways the old Soviet regimes could only dream of: though citizens may feel empowered by, or at least addicted to, their äppäräti, their integration with these devices makes them vulnerable to constant surveillance and coercion. So powerful is the äppärät that separation from it triggers something like an existential crisis. When the devices are disabled during the novel's concluding civil strife, Eunice struggles to adapt to a noncommercial identity: "In the living room, [she] had opened up her äppärät and was concentrating on the last shopping page stored in its memory before communications collapsed. I could see she had instinctively opened a LandOLakes Credit Payment stream, but every time she tried to input her account info, she ended up throwing her head back as if stung. 'I can't buy anything,' she said."[40] Others find themselves unable to go on without the technology's reassuring orientations: "Four young people committed suicide in our building complexes, and two of them wrote suicide notes about how they couldn't see a future without their äppäräti. One wrote, quite eloquently, about how he 'reached out to life,' but found there only 'walls and thoughts and faces,' which weren't enough. He needed to be ranked, to know his place in this world."[41]

In *The Age of Intelligent Machines* (1990), Ray Kurzweil, whom Shteyngart had studied closely in researching *Super Sad,* noted how newly emerging technology might make possible much more thorough forms of state tyranny. His cautious prediction at the end of the twentieth century, however, was that capitalist forces would, at least to some extent, work to democratize the liberating potential of whatever inventions arise: "Computer technology may lead to a flowering of individual expression, creativity, and communication or to an era of efficient and effective totalitarian control. It will all depend on who controls the technology. A hopeful note is that the nature of wealth and power in the age of intelligent machines will encourage the open society. Oppressive societies will find it hard to provide the economic incentives needed to pay for computers and their development."[42] In Shteyngart's rankly overripe and miserably discordant America, capitalism and totalitarianism have merged to produce a society that is at once open, seemingly offering its citizens nearly unlimited freedoms, and yet definitively closed, as those freedoms can be expressed only within an environment of relentless public exposure and punitive control.[43]

Shteyngart's satire of the coercive power of others' judgments extends a critique articulated nearly two centuries ago by the famous French observer of American life, Alexis de Tocqueville. Egalitarianism, de Tocqueville argued, elevates "the public" into "a singular power, . . . for it does not persuade to certain opinions, but it enforces them, and infuses them into the faculties by a sort of enormous pressure of the minds of all upon the reason of each."[44] Under the banner of universal access to the pursuit of happiness, citizens in fact submit themselves to the whims of a hypervigilant and hypercritical tyranny of the masses. As de Tocqueville prophesied, such conditions form a new godhead in the imagined impression one is making on others: "by whatever political laws men are governed in the ages of equality, it may be foreseen that faith in public opinion will become a species of religion there, and the majority its ministering prophet."[45] Shteyngart has given us a United States in which this curious paradox discerned by de Tocqueville—a rather craven dependence upon others' opinions in the land of "rugged individualism"—has metastasized, with the growth of means to create and gauge publicity, into an outright negation of the nation's mythic commitment to personal autonomy. In other words one pursues one's liberty by slavishly, "religiously" tracking and conforming oneself to the prophetic values and expectations of an imagined mass of others.

If all spaces have become common, the public *sensibility* reigning there is common too—reduced to a sort of adolescent vulgarity, *poshlost* in its tawdriest colors. Shteyngart wrote in his memoir of the infantilizing dynamics of political allegiances: "The goal of politics is to make us children. The more heinous the system the more this is true. The Soviet system worked best when its adults—its men, in particular—were welcomed to stay at the emotional level of not-particularly-advanced teenagers."[46] *Super Sad True Love Story*'s citizens function precisely at this level or even a little below it. Much social interaction in the novel is dedicated to determining fellow citizens' "Fuckability,"[47] an endlessly anatomized measure of self-worth, and much social expression is marked by relentless provocativeness: Noah "pointed the clumped remains of his frontal hair at me and said: 'All right, here's the situation, Nee-gro. You have to fuck either Mother Teresa or Margaret Thatcher.'"[48] Commercial enterprises reflect and drive this vulgarization, offering products with names such as JuicyPussy and AssLuxury. Lenny, as an early middle-aged man, is at his most vulnerable and pathetic in his attempts to fit in with youth culture and win the affection of Eunice, its chief emblem. Her prose style in many of her communications, especially early in the novel, suggests the basic crudity of this culture, its routine sensationalism and corrosive irony: "What's up, twat? Missing your 'tard? Wanna dump a little sugar on me? JBF. I am so sick of making out with girls. BTW, I saw the pictures on the Elderbird alum board with your tongue in Bryana's, um, ear. I hope you're not trying to get Gopher jealous? He's had way too many threesomes. Respect yourself, hoo-kah!"[49] Crassly eroticized commercialism even shapes religious services, which seem to have merged with the entertainment industry:

> The service began. A cellist, two oboists, several violinists, a pianist, and a small, adorable choir, the majority of them young women dressed in rather form-fitting gowns, mounted the stage and began to play a medley of songs that varied between the sacred and the bizarre. We got a Mahler

> violin concerto, then the stirring Korean pop anthem Alphaville's "Forever Young" sung by some exhausted-looking teenagers in bad haircuts and tight jeans, which they followed with a power-rock tribute to Ephesians that left the older half of the congregation visibly confused. We ended with "Softly and Tenderly Jesus is Calling." It was this last song that roused all the parishioners who began to sing loudly and with gusto as a kind of PowerPoint presentation appeared on a large screen in both Korean and English against a backdrop of orchids floating down streams and a very visible copyright sign, which seemed to soothe our law-abiding natures.[50]

There is little in this world, in other words, that has not been thoroughly prostituted.

In chasing after Eunice, Lenny evokes Humbert Humbert from Vladimir Nabokov's *Lolita,* a novel whose own send-up of youth culture and American *poshlost* seems to be a major influence on Shteyngart. Though she is about a decade older, Eunice evokes Nabokov's tragic heroine with her prepubescent physique ("desperately trying to coax out the preliminaries of an adult body"),[51] troubled family life, and thralldom to consumer culture. Like Lolita, Eunice is vulnerable to a paternal figure who can offer her the love and security her own father has failed to provide; Lenny's attempts to fill this role parallel Humbert's, as he clumsily tries to camouflage himself in youth culture in order to win her approval. Lenny seems like a less vicious, more sympathetic, nerdier version of Humbert, with his boss Joshie standing in for Clare Quilty, the quasi-doppelganger who is, in contrast to what Lenny sees as his own purer motives, "clearly guilty" of the exploitation of innocence. Shteyngart's satirical suggestion here, like Nabokov's in *Lolita,* is that youth culture is at least in some ways only *seemingly* arranged according to the interests of the young; its essential consumer dynamics are in fact fundamentally predatory on youth and aligned with the interests of powerful older men. As Humbert relates of his entrapment of Lolita after her mother dies, leaving her utterly dependent on him:

> In the gay town of Lepingville I bought her four books of comics, a box of candy, a box of sanitary pads, two cokes, a manicure set, a travel clock with a luminous dial, a ring with a real topaz, a tennis racket, roller skates with white high shoes, field glasses, a portable radio set, chewing gum, a transparent raincoat, sunglasses, some more garments—swooners, shorts, all kinds of summer frocks. At the hotel we had separate rooms, but in the middle of the night she came sobbing into mine, and we made it up very gently. You see, she had absolutely nowhere else to go.[52]

In a somewhat-less-sinister way, Lenny similarly conspires to woo his lover through her dependence, for at least initially he has the financial resources to support her as she evades her overbearing family. He will "bait [Eunice] to New York,"[53] then secure his position by ingratiating himself with the other authority figures who he realizes still control his young lover's life: "The parents were the key to Eunice Park."[54]

Lenny's love of books is laughable and even somewhat suspicious among those who "scan text" rather than read, and he struggles to accommodate himself to the truncated, vulgarized expression now used in the age of social networking:

> "LPT," she said. "TIMATOV. ROFLAARP. PRGV. Totally PRGV."
>
> The youth and their abbreviations. I pretended like I knew what she was talking about. "Right," I said. "IMF. PLO. ESL."
>
> She looked at me like I was insane. "JBF," she said.
>
> "Who's that?" I pictured a tall Protestant man.
>
> "It means I'm 'just butt-fucking' with you. Just kidding, you know."[55]

Though he is in full pursuit of Eunice and tries to adapt himself to her world, Lenny still belongs in part to a generation that cherishes language, not unlike Humbert, who is a professor of English and French literature, which he sometimes attempts to read to Lolita. Lenny's apartment contains a "Wall of Books"—a secular alternative perhaps to the Wailing Wall—where he carries out an idiosyncratic form of "worship": "'You're my sacred ones,' I told the books. 'No one but me still cares about you. But I'm going to keep you with me forever. And one day I'll make you important again.'"[56] This cultural inheritance gives him a certain depth, in contrast to the contemporary world's ahistorical youth, who are typically preoccupied with quickly consumable images rather than difficult-to-digest text. As in *Little Failure,* in which Shteyngart wrote about the end of the twentieth century—when Lenny was presumably Eunice's age—the last two decades had seen a broad decline in reading and with it a deterioration of the rich subjectivity that immersion in literature can provide: "In 1996, people still read books and the city could support an extra branch of the legendary Strand in the Financial District, which is to say that stockbrokers, secretaries, government functionaries—everybody back then was expected to have some inner life."[57] In the twenty-first-century world of *Super Sad,* an increasing self-absorption paradoxically has exposed and emptied much of citizens' inner lives. This leaves Lenny stranded in the still-recent past, his love of books becoming an embarrassing sign for his peers of his failure to evolve, to open himself to the present. Insulted by a young coworker, he frames his experience according to his literary knowledge, which merges with or reaffirms his sense of inferiority: "Momentarily, I saw Chekhov's prose before my eyes, his description of the Moscow merchant's son Laptev [from the novella "Three Years"], who 'knew that he was ugly, and now he felt as though he was conscious of his ugliness all over his body.'"[58]

Near the novel's end, Lenny affirms that a care for language is essential to thinking and living well, to organizing one's memories and appreciating the world's sensuous variety: "A month ago, mid-October, a gust of autumnal wind kicked its way down Grand Street. A co-op woman, old, tired, Jewish, fake drops of jade spread across the little sacks of her bosom, looked up at the pending wind and said one word: 'Blustery.' Just one word, a word meaning no more than 'a period of time characterized by strong winds,' but it caught me unaware, it reminded me of how language was once used, its precision and simplicity, its capacity for recall."[59] The passage seems to emphasize both Lenny's virtues and his limitations, especially in relation to Eunice. On the one hand, he preserves a sense of the potency of language, in spite of the contemporary world's indifference, and can locate its value even when it emerges from unglamorous, even *poshlost* sources, as in the "fake drops of jade spread across the little sacks of [the woman's] bosom." On the other hand, Lenny's focus on the word itself in this memory, his primary interest in its message about what language can do for individual perception, also seems to signal his own inability to think beyond himself and to connect language to traditions that even in a debased age might continue to connect people—characteristically, it is just the word that attracts his curiosity here, not the woman, nor indeed her "Jewishness."

Though Lenny is, much like Vladimir Girshkin and Misha Vainberg, overtly cynical about organized religion, he does seem to yearn for—while mourning the impossibility of it—a kind of language that might unite people according to a common, transcendent purpose. During a long set-piece in which he attends a church service with Eunice and her family, he admires—while condescending to—Christianity's belief in, and care for, the aesthetic power of words:

> I was caught unawares by the line "Why should we tarry when Jesus is pleading? / Pleading for you and for me?" The English language was dying around us, Christianity was as unsatisfying and delusional an idea as it had ever been, but the effectiveness of the sentence—its clever mix of kitsch, guilt, and heartbreaking imagery, Jesus *pleading* for the attention and love of these put-upon Asian people—made me shudder. The awful thing was: They were beautiful words. For the first time in my life, I felt sorry for Jesus. Sorry that the miracles ascribed to him hadn't actually made a difference.

> Sorry that we were all alone in a universe where even our fathers would let us get nailed to a tree if they were so inclined, or cut our throats if so commanded—see under Isaac, another unfortunate Jewish shmuck.[60]

In response to a sermon delivered by a man named Reverend Suk that urges humility and the cultivation of shame, Lenny affirms a pride in the human: "You are better than this angry man," he wants to tell the parishioners, "You are better than Jesus Christ."[61] Shame, argues Lenny in a heated rejection of the sermon's message, is a Jewish invention, foolishly adopted by Christianity, and it ought to be abandoned as part of a vigorous spiritual housecleaning:

> Get up off your knees. Do not throw away your heart. Keep your heart. Your heart is all that matters. Throw away your shame! Throw away your modesty! Throw away your ancestors! Throw away your fathers and the self-appointed fathers that claim to be stewards of God. Throw away your shyness and the anger that lies just a few inches beneath. Do not believe the Judeo-Christian lie! Accept your thoughts! Accept your desires! Accept the truth! And if there is more than one truth, then learn to do the difficult work—learn to choose. You are good enough, you are *human enough*, to choose![62]

Among the prominent ironies here is that Lenny is himself a "worshipper" of his boss, Joshie ("Jesus"), from whom he seeks a spiritual deliverance every bit as abject as that he mocks in the Parks's church: "But I just wanted to listen to him take care of me some more. I wanted him to pay close attention to my dihydrotestosterone and to rescue me from the beautiful bullies in the Eternity Lounge. . . . I am still a facsimile of my early childhood. I am still looking for a loving dad to lift me up and brush the sand off my ass and to hear English, calm and hurtless, fall off his lips."[63] Moreover, Lenny's exhortations to self-acceptance and a severance from ancestral authorities hardly seem distinct from the general tendencies of äppärät culture, which would have all its networked apparatchiks indulge and celebrate their own ostensibly self-generated desires, the only significant difference perhaps being that he would somehow suspend any anxious dependence on *other's* acceptance of one's own self-celebrations.

Lenny's professed humanism—which is much more representative of the novel's mainstream culture than is the Parks's Christianity—would leave behind organized religion in favor of what he characterizes as a sober, rational belief in the power of individuals to find meaning on their own. As he unself-consciously suggests after seeing a woman crossing herself outside a church, worldly commitments are better than supernal ones: "I wanted to confront her, to make her see the folly of her religion, to change her diet, to help her spend less on makeup and other nonessentials, to make her worship every biological moment she was offered instead of some badly punctured deity."[64] The Pantheon (Greek, "all gods") is, he tells us, his favorite building: "When I outlive the earth and depart from its familiar womb, I will take [its memory] with me. I will encode it with zeros and ones and broadcast it across the universe. See what primitive man has wrought! Witness his first hankerings for immortality, his discipline, his selflessness."[65] Lenny's reverence for this building is hardly selfless in its implications, to be sure, for he would participate in an effective self-deification, which is the essential promise of äppärät culture, thus elevating himself—in fulfilment of his name-fate as an "Abram"—among the gods in his beloved temple. His workplace at Post-Human Services is in fact "housed in a former Moorish-style synagogue near Fifth Avenue,"[66] suggesting a new human presumption to divinity and, as ever, its commercial exploitation.

One of the slogans of Lenny's corporation declares that "NATURE HAS A LOT TO LEARN FROM US,"[67] for these technologies promise the utter domination of the natural world, and all "natural" processes, by the human will. These brazen, hubristic experiments with the pastoral—aimed at returning humans, or at least a select number of them, to paradise—open up a Gothic potential, and retell the ancient story refashioned in Mary Shelley's *Frankenstein; or, the Modern Prometheus.* In his memoir Shteyngart spoke of his fascination as a child with the television series *The Six Million Dollar Man* and his perception of its ultimate message: "After all, this is America, and you can swap out the parts of yourself that don't work. You can rebuild yourself piece by piece."[68] Michael Wood's review of *Super Sad True Love Story* aptly points out another Gothic type at play here: "There is a would-be vampire story lurking in the science fiction."[69] Joshie, Lenny's eventual rival for the love of Eunice, is the novel's presiding vampire, although of course Lenny has his own vampiric qualities too. A septuagenarian who has physically rejuvenated himself through "dechronification treatments," Joshie now looks forty years younger than his chronological age and has adopted the speech patterns of a twenty-something hipster. His name links him to the biblical Joshua, who was granted invincibility during his lifetime as successor to Moses and leader of the Israelites. Selling technologies that promise immortality, Joshie becomes a new kind of deliverer of a chosen people—the wealthy—to a new kind of promised land, eternal youth. Significantly he does not carry an äppärät, for this aspiring vampire thwarts the reflections of the contemporary world's mirror.

Gothic tropes are most explicitly deployed during a visit that Lenny, as the unknowing procurer, and Eunice, as the vulnerable maiden, make to Joshie's apartment, which can be seen as a version of the villain's ancient, haunted castle. The décor there suggests Joshie's frozenness in boyhood: "Posters from his youth—science-fiction films with big-haired women and deep-jawed men. . . . The names alone. *Soylent Green. Logan's Run.* Here were [his] beginnings. A dystopian upper-class childhood in several elite American suburbs. Total immersion in *Isaac Asimov's Science Fiction Magazine.* The twelve-year-old's first cognition of mortality, for the true subject of science fiction is death, not life."[70] Among the other peculiar decorations in the apartment are photographs of a one-man play called *Sins of the Mother* and a "watercolor of an old, naked woman [his mother] shattered into three by an unnamed force, her empty breasts flying in all directions, a dark pubic mound holding the thirds together."[71] This display amounts to something like the demonic epicentre of the narrative's exploration of *poshlost*—a grotesque, Oedipal perversity cloyingly presented as maternal reverence. The symbolic implication is that Joshie's quest to overcome mortality would have him at last interfere with Mother Nature herself.

Joshie also seems to evoke a sort of contemporary, more obviously corrupt Jay Gatsby. Lenny relates that "when Joshie looked at you, when he lowered his gaze at you, the heat would rise in your cheeks and you would find yourself oddly, irrevocably present,"[72] a seeming analogue to the way Nick Carraway, whom Lenny resembles in his initial fawning over Joshie, describes Gatsby's charisma: "He smiled understandingly—much more than understandingly. It was one of those rare smiles with a quality of eternal reassurance in it, that you may come across four or five times in life. It faced—or seemed to face—the whole eternal world for an instant, and then concentrated on *you* with an irresistible prejudice in your favour."[73] Joshie, himself dedicated to "the whole eternal world," is a twinkling representative of the American commitment to redeeming history, having spent his adult life "devoting himself to one idea,"[74] now personified by the youthful Eunice. He would, like Gatsby, refuse to submit to the tyranny of time:

> [Gatsby] broke off and began to walk up and down a desolate path of fruit rinds and discarded favors and crushed flowers.
>
> 'I wouldn't ask too much of her,' I ventured. 'You can't repeat the past.'
>
> 'Can't repeat the past?' he cried incredulously. 'Why of course you can!'
>
> He looked around him wildly, as if the past were lurking there in the shadow of his house, just out of reach of his hand.
>
> 'I'm going to fix everything just the way it was before,' he said, nodding determinedly. 'She'll see.'
>
> He talked a lot about the past and I gathered that he wanted to recover something, some idea of himself perhaps, that had gone into loving Daisy.[75]

Gatsby's predatory romanticism—his exploitation of others in the pursuit of his personal fantasy—becomes explicit (and patently ridiculous) in Joshie, whose "love" has an obviously coercive dimension. In a love letter to Eunice, Joshie makes clear both his own senile adolescence and the viciousness lurking behind his romantic promises, also characteristic of Kundera's totalitarian *kitsch:*

> How does your smile reduce one of the most powerful men in the hemisphere to a dopey teenager? It's like I feel that together we can redeem whatever misery we encountered on this planet, whatever awfulness we faced as children.
>
> Anyway, I feel so totally, like, weird opening up my heart like this to you, because what I feel for YOU and for YOUR FAMILY IN FORT LEE AND THEIR WELL-BEING, is so strong and without reservation, that I fear it might make you run away from me.[76]

While selling the promise of eternal youth through his enormously powerful corporation, Joshie helps organize the removal of the poor and vulnerable from New York, a replaying not just of the biblical Joshua's bloody campaigns against the people of Canaan, but of a foundational American story, the displacement and genocide of Native Americans by European colonists.[77] Note here another correspondence with Kundera's *The Unbearable Lightness of Being* and its own diagnosis of the hubris, and potential for violence, lurking within totalitarianism. As Kundera wrote, "Anyone who thinks that the Communist regimes of Central Europe are exclusively the work of criminals is overlooking a basic truth: the criminal regimes were made not by criminals but by enthusiasts convinced they had discovered the only road to paradise. They defended that road so valiantly that they were forced to execute many people. Later it became clear that there was no paradise, that the enthusiasts were therefore murderers."[78]

As America descends into chaos during the novel's concluding stages, Joshie addresses his employees with appeals to the nation's historic ideals. The poor and vulnerable must be eliminated, he tells them, "Because we are the last, best hope for this nation's future."[79] Joshie borrows here a famous phrase uttered by Thomas Jefferson—in his first inaugural address he proudly and resonantly dubbed the United States "the world's best hope"[80]—which was itself modified by Abraham Lincoln in his 1862 State of the Union address: "In *giving* freedom to the *slave,* we *assure* freedom to the *free*—honorable alike in what we give, and what we preserve. We shall nobly save, or meanly lose, the last best hope of earth."[81] Joshie lacks the grand idealism of Jefferson and Lincoln, of course, since it is not an entire nation's interests that he claims to defend, but rather those of his corporation and its wealthy clients. He in effect suggests that this defense ought to proceed "by any means necessary," further draining *that* phrase—which was deployed in *The Russian Debutante's Handbook* as a touchstone of Jewish survival and in *Absurdistan* as a surrender to cynical selfishness—of its ethical weight. Joshie's efforts at "dechronification" ultimately fail as the technology proves flawed, and by the novel's end he is himself borne back ceaselessly into the past, reduced to a frail, elderly man. Lenny, like Shteyngart's previous two protagonists, ultimately lands in a sort of cultural sanctuary: the post-Rupture version of Italy now known as the Tuscan Free State, a "place with less data, less youth, and where old people like myself were not despised simply for being old."[82] He will mourn here the fact that "*America's gone.*"[83] This conclusion suggests the ultimate decline of American pastoral mythologies—which, as Fitzgerald wrote, once "pandered in whispers to the last and greatest of all human dreams"[84]—and the apocalyptic transformation of the nation into a Gothic dystopia.

In an unsympathetic review of *Super Sad,* Ruth Franklin contended that the novel is finally unsuccessful in conveying a sense of importance in the love story it tells, particularly in regard to its female protagonist: "Eunice is a digital creature to her core, her mind little more than a pastiche of advertising images: how could she be expected to express an authentic emotion?"[85] Given her absorption in popular, commercial culture, and the distracted life she leads on her äppärät, Eunice may indeed strike many readers as simply a cipher—or as something like the not-quite-human "pastiche" Humbert Humbert initially takes Lolita for: "She it was to whom ads were dedicated: the ideal consumer, the subject and object of every foul poster."[86]

These verdicts, however, seem unfair. Part of *Super Sad True Love Story*'s importance can be found in the vivid job it does mapping out the manifold hazards facing *any* lovers in the contemporary age. The novel shows us a nation itself committed to obsessive and trivialized self-exaltation, a technologically aided narcissism that makes it difficult to love beyond the self, just as one of Humbert's problems is an inability to acknowledge Lolita's subjectivity as distinct from his own fantasies. Radical and relentless self-exposure and self-promotion contribute, Shteyngart has suggested, to a loss of the sacred or "set apart" quality of love. When Eunice's mother fruitlessly and comically cautions her daughter about the importance of sexual restraint—"Do not give away mystery"[87]—she voices not just a bit of homely advice for negotiating marriage, but a compelling and finally unironic indictment of the hedonism and permissiveness that have ultimately diminished contemporary erotic life.

Moreover, the novel makes clear early on the significance of Eunice's potential to be nourished, unlike Lenny, by her cultural heritage. As Humbert

Humbert says of Lolita, in his belated acknowledgement of what his own self-absorption has obscured, a rich and precious subjectivity can exist within the *poshlost* world that frames it: "it struck me . . . that I simply did not know a thing about my darling's mind and that quite possibly, behind the awful juvenile clichés, there was in her a garden and a twilight, and a palace gate—dim and adorable regions which happened to be lucidly and absolutely forbidden to me."[88] When Eunice is first introduced, she has been volunteering to help exploited women in Italy, an activity that Lenny tellingly ignores and misunderstands. By the end of the book, her charitable impulses have slowly but dramatically bloomed, as she demonstrates a genuine commitment to others (as does, perhaps even more surprisingly, her father). The elderly are despised by Lenny—"Maybe I hated all the old people in my building, and wished them to disappear already so that I could focus on my own struggle with mortality"[89]—whose devotion to eternal life seems like a logical projection of his own core narcissism. He has effectively cut himself off from his ethnic heritage in his self-devotion—committing himself, like Misha Vainberg, to survival "by any means necessary"—as he concedes while watching Eunice wash the feet of their aged neighbors: "I feared one day having to care for my parents in so thoughtful and tactile a manner, as Russian tradition expected of me—but Eunice, who despised any alien smell coming from our refrigerator or the rankness of my toenails after several missed pedicures, did not flinch, did not turn away from the sunken, splotched flesh in her hands."[90] Unlike her wholly ahistorical peers, she can know who she is through her connection to a communal past: "America might be gone completely soon, but I was never really an American. It was all pretending. I was always a Korean girl from a Korean family with a Korean way of doing things, and I'm proud of what that means. It means that, unlike so many people around me, I know who I am."[91] Morgan and Rouenna are hardly more than foils in *The Russian Debutante's Handbook* and *Absurdistan*, but Eunice is ultimately a fully articulated character—one whose rounded humanity emerges by the novel's end, earning her, as her own name-fate would suggest, an unironic "good/well-achieved victory" in an otherwise defeated world.

CHAPTER 5

Little Failure

The YouTube trailer for *Little Failure* reintroduces us to a burlesqued version of Shteyngart's authorial persona: now apparently literate but retaining something of the thickly accented, disheveled buffoon encountered in the *Super Sad True Love Story* trailers.[1] James Franco appears here once again—playing the role of the author's fawning but ambitious "husband"—along with cameos by fellow novelist Jonathan Franzen and actors Rashida Jones and Alex Karpovsky. At a meeting with his editors at the corporate headquarters of Random House, "Shteyngart" is informed that a focus group associates him with the words "little," given his small stature, and "failure," given the general impression he makes. Further comic humiliations follow, including a diagnosis of narcissism by his text-messaging psychotherapist, played by Franzen, and the news that his work has been overshadowed by Franco's acclaimed tell-all—an erotic memoir called *50 Shades of Gary.*

The starpower of this advertisement suggests Shteyngart's prominent status as a literary celebrity and droll entertainer at this stage of his career. While the memoir itself is often comic, it finally aims for a realism and seriousness that seem quite distinct from the farcical bent of the author's novels and indeed of the trailer itself. *Little Failure* seeks to drop the buffoonish accent, as it were, and earnestly describe the actual conditions of personal and communal dysfunction that lie behind the fiction. Structured according to a series of flashbacks, the memoir takes us through the extraordinary suffering endured by Shteyngart's ancestors over the past century, his family's immigration to the United States from Leningrad when he was a young child, his gradual and often-tortured acculturation in New York, and finally his ascent to literary celebrity by the time he reaches his late twenties. A central mystery organizes the author's survey of his own life history: the source of a panic attack that he had endured after leafing through a coffee-table book devoted to the architecture of St. Petersburg (formerly Leningrad) in 1996. The memoir's final chapter solved that mystery, as Shteyngart described a revelatory trip with his parents, in 2011, back to present-day St. Petersburg.

Little Failure was joined in 2014 by an extraordinary number of other fiction and nonfiction titles by Russian, and particularly Jewish Russian, Americans—prompting the book reviewer Yevgeniya Traps to remark that this was "the year of the Soviet American Jew, when it seems like every man, woman and child who hails from the good old USSR and owns a writing implement has detailed his or her experience, fictionally or otherwise."[2] Shteyngart has led the way in popularizing twenty-first-century Russian American literature, and his memoir was part of a continuing great harvest from the "beet generation," to use Emily Gould's witty term for a group of Russian American authors—with Shteyngart as its most high-profile member—who rose to prominence in the last decade or so.[3] Memoirs from "beets" have been particularly strong in the last several years. Elena Gorokhova's *A Mountain of Crumbs* appeared in 2010, and its follow-up, *A Russian Tattoo,* in early 2015. As her publisher's summary suggests, Gorokhova's works tell a story in many ways similar to Shteyngart's: "In *A Mountain of Crumbs,* [the author] describes coming of age behind the Iron Curtain and leaving her mother and her Motherland for a new life in the United States. Now, in *Russian Tattoo,* Elena learns that the journey of an immigrant is filled with everyday mistakes, small humiliations, and a loss of dignity."[4] Lev Golinkin's memoir *A Backpack, a Bear, and Eight Crates of Vodka,* which appeared several months after *Little Failure,* is likened on the Penguin site to works by a series of authors with Russian credentials: "Written with biting, acerbic wit and emotional honesty in the vein of Gary Shteyngart, Jonathan Safran Foer, and David Bezmozgis, Golinkin's search for personal identity set against the relentless currents of history is more than a memoir—it's a portrait of a lost era."[5] As Alexandra Tatarsky wryly noted of the seductive mystique of Russian authorial identities: "if the [publishers'] blurbs are to believed, contemporary Russian American authors all write like Tolstoy/Dostoevsky/ Chekhov/Gogol/Babel/Nabokov, carrying the blessing and burden of their literary heritage."[6]

A number of popular nonfiction works exploring the social problems facing contemporary Russia also appeared around the time of *Little Failure*'s publication, confirming an enduring Western curiosity about the evolving conditions of post-Soviet life. David Greene's *Midnight in Siberia: A Train Journey into the Heart of Russia* (2014) is advertised as offering a glimpse of "the new Russia—a nation that boasts open elections and newfound prosperity but continues to endure oppression, corruption, a dwindling population, and stark inequality."[7] Peter Pomerantsev's *Nothing Is True and Everything Is Possible: The Surreal Heart of the New Russia* is pitched, much more colorfully, as an exploration of a failed state remarkably similar to the farcical and grotesque worlds of *The Russian Debutante's Handbook* and *Absurdistan:*

> In the new Russia, even dictatorship is a reality show. Professional killers with the souls of artists, would-be theater directors turned Kremlin puppet-masters, suicidal supermodels, Hell's Angels who hallucinate themselves as holy warriors, and oligarch revolutionaries: welcome to the glittering, surreal heart of twenty-first-century Russia. It is a world erupting with new money and new power, changing so fast it breaks all sense of reality, home to a form of dictatorship—far subtler than twentieth-century strains—that is rapidly rising to challenge the West.
>
> When British producer Peter Pomerantsev plunges into the booming Russian TV industry, he gains access to every nook and corrupt cranny of the country. He is brought to smoky rooms for meetings with propaganda gurus running the nerve-center of the Russian media machine, and visits Siberian mafia-towns and the salons of the international super-rich in London and the US. As the Putin regime becomes more aggressive, Pomerantsev finds himself drawn further into the system.[8]

In such works the mystique of the Russian past and the ostensibly lurid conditions of the Russian present combine to make a highly marketable literary commodity.

Appraisals of *Little Failure* have typically hinged on its blending of the tragic and comic. Andy Borowitz called the book "hilarious and moving," noting its undeniable rage, which, he suggested, is "part of what makes [it] so compelling."[9] For Meg Wolitzer, "Shteyngart's humor comes out of the most serious material, and vice versa."[10] Jennie Yabroff has contended that the "success of [the memoir] is Shteyngart's scrupulous examination of the chasm between his parents' experiences and his own, and his hard-won understanding of the way his family's murky, bloody, half-understood history informs his present."[11] A dissenting opinion was expressed by Randy Boyagoda:

> The greater challenge of *Little Failure* concerns Shteyngart's ultimate ambition to be taken seriously, even solemnly: the final section is an account of a trip to Russia . . . [which] exposes family secrets and inspires moving confessions of regret and love. It's fine stuff, but because of how frequently, and finally tiresomely, Shteyngart bends the serious into the satirical and silly elsewhere in the book, you find yourself waiting for the literary equivalent

> of a whoopee cushion to go off. In the end there are no cheap jokes, only a very talented writer risking far more than he has prepared you to expect, which is, alas, its own kind of *Failurchka*.[12]

Shteyngart's interest in staking his claim to the serious is suggested late in the memoir by his dismissal of his first novel, which he described as "a collection of increasingly desperate jokes."[13] He noted ruefully that "to this day, some people tell me it's my best work, implying that it's all been kind of a downhill slog from there."[14] This decline is presumably from largely light-hearted farce (*The Russian Debutante's Handbook*), to a more nuanced form of caricature that attempts to register the existence of grave realities behind distorted surfaces (*Absurdistan*), to a much more earnest and pointed satire (*Super Sad True Love Story*) that allows ample space, amid its own panorama of comic grotesques, for realistic representations of human suffering. In an interview with Michael Hafford, Shteyngart emphasized the obligation he felt to go further in his memoir than he had in his often highly autobiographical fiction, presenting his life honestly without obscuring painful truths with clowning:

> For me, the most important thing was doing it right. But there's a kind of safety net that comes with writing a satire. You can do humor, humor, humor, something sad, humor, humor, humor, something sad. But the way life is lived, it's not going to fall into that three-to-one, three-to-one trajectory. If you've had this kind of life, you're not going to be able to hide behind humor as you are in a satire. Otherwise, it's going to come out as disjointed or it's going to come out as a sad attempt to make your audience laugh.[15]

A common trait among the male protagonists of Shteyngart's novels is the delusive—if sympathetically rendered—conviction that the errors and miseries of the past can somehow be miraculously redeemed in the present. Vladimir Girshkin would transform himself into the authentic Russian, or the authentic American, that a different childhood might have easily let him become. Misha Vainberg would reverse the wounding separations of his father's Judaism in merging with the American multicultural mosaic, overcoming marginality with undiscriminating consumption. Lenny Abramov and, even more extremely, his mentor Joshie Goldman, would finally reverse a lifetime's disappointments and a steady slide into obsolescence by claiming eternal youthfulness. A frequent satirical target in Shteyngart's fiction too is the institutionalized form of such blinkered optimism, which traps adherents, he contended in *Little Failure,* in a dangerous and deranging misconception: "The terrible thing about the major belief systems (Leninism, Christianity) is that too often they are constructed along the premise that a difficult past can be traded in for a better future, that all adversity leads to triumph, either through the installation of telegraph poles (Leninism) or at Jesus' knee after physical death (Christianity). But the past is not simply redeemable for a better future."[16] The yearning of his protagonists for a radical emancipation from the past, and the selves chained to it, has often been his own, Shteyngart confirmed, but, in searching for the origins of familial suffering and dysfunction in the memoir, he can approach his personal history with a sort of qualified hopefulness, a chastened awareness that the past cannot be magically transfigured but only better understood, better tolerated.

Shteyngart's personal history in *Little Failure*—from asthmatic Leningrad youngster to emergent New York novelist—is framed by much darker stories. Relatives on both sides of his family were bludgeoned by some of the twentieth century's greatest catastrophes, leaving a legacy of suffering still acutely insistent today. On his father's side, there was persecution and deprivation:

> The Stone Horns [as the Shteyngarts were once known] inhabit the Ukrainian town of Chemirovets, where my father's paternal grandfather was killed for no good reason in the 1920s. My father's grandmother was left to fend for herself and a family of five children. There was not enough to eat. Those who could went up to Leningrad, Russia's former imperial capital and second most important city once the Bolsheviks crowned Moscow as the capital. There, they mostly died, too. They were a deeply religious clan, but the Soviets took that from them as well, before they took what little else remained.[17]

And on his mother's side there was more trauma and desolation: "One bitter Eastern European night, Great-grandpa Miller is riding home with a great deal of Jewish money in his saddlebag, when one of the many criminal bands roaming freely across the Ukraine in the chaos following the 1917 Revolution murders him. The Millers are ruined."[18] Stalin and Hitler would combine to eliminate much of the rest of the two families: "My great-grandmother sends her starving seven-year-old daughter, Fenya, to an orphanage in Leningrad. Fenya and my grandmother are among the three Miller siblings out of nine who will survive World War II. Some will die fighting at the front against the invading Germans; some will die at the hands of the SS and their Ukrainian colleagues; at least one will, poignantly, 'lose her mind,' according to my father, and die before the war even gets properly started."[19]

Shteyngart's parents—his mother taught piano at a kindergarten, and his father worked as a mechanical engineer—enjoyed a more stable and prosperous life than their own parents, but by the late 1970s they were ready to leave the Soviet Union with their young son. In 1978, when Shteyngart was six, they took advantage of a program allowing Soviet Jews to leave the country: "the American president Jimmy Carter has reached a deal with the Russians. In exchange for tons of grain and some high technology, the USSR will allow many of its Jews to leave. Russia gets the grain it needs to run; America gets the Jews it needs to run: all in all, an excellent trade deal."[20] After stops in Vienna and Rome, the Shteyngarts arrived in Queens, New York, which stunned the young Igor, as he was known before adopting the more American-friendly "Gary," with its kaleidoscopic immensity:

> 1979. Coming to America after a childhood spent in the Soviet Union is equivalent to stumbling off a monochromatic cliff and landing in a pool of pure Technicolor. . . . The sweep of what used to be JFK's Pan Am terminal with its "flying saucer" roof and, above, the expanse of sky that doesn't press down on Queen's, as the Russian sky tramples Leningrad, but flows past in waves, allotting a bit of itself to each red-bricked or aluminum-sided house and to each of the lucky families that dwells within. . . . The intensity of arrival will not abate. Everything is revelation. On the ride from the airport, I am shocked by my first highway overpass, the way the car (a private car bigger than three Soviet Ladas) leans into the curve hundreds of feet above the greenery of Queens. Here we are floating through air but in a car.[21]

Blessed for several years by the absence of a television, Shteyngart read voraciously in Russian, while slowly coming to comprehend the popular culture and diverse peoples of New York. Though it would be a number of years before his family reached a secure middle-class status, one of his earliest discoveries about his new home was its consumerist promises: "In America the distance between wanting something and having it delivered to your living room is not terribly great."[22]

Even casual readers have noted the seeming closeness of much of Shteyngart's fiction to the material of his own life, an impression often reinforced by his interviews as well as the promotional material accompanying his books. Vladimir in *The Russian Debutante's Handbook*, though obviously a creature of fantasy, seems like the nearest to Shteyngart himself. The two have roughly similar biographies and share a defining sense of cultural dividedness. Like Vladimir's parents, the Shteyngarts preserved a sort of "Little Leningrad" in their home while advancing in their American careers: "Except for Leon Uris and his tales of Israeli derring-do, our house is Russian down to the last buckwheat kernel of kasha. English is the language of commerce and work, but Russian is the language of the soul, whatever that is. . . . The reason I still speak, think, dream, and quake in fear in Russian has to do with my parents' dictum that only Russian be spoken in the home. It's a trade-off. While I will retain my Russian, my parents will struggle with the new language, nothing being more instructive than having a child prattle on in English at the dinner table."[23] Multiple episodes from Shteyngart's own experiences at Oberlin College make their way into *Absurdistan,* along with some undoubtedly invented ones, as do memories of his parents in his representation of the elder Abramovs in *Super Sad True Love Story.* In preparing to write *Little Failure,* he reread his novels and was surprised to find so many correspondences with his own experience: "[The] exercise left me shocked . . . by how blithely I've used the facts of my own life, as if I've been having a fire sale all along—everything about me must go!"[24] A sense of cowardice shadowed his reading as well, for he admitted that his novels would sometimes draw close to a disturbing reality only to "scurry back to safety."[25] In the memoir, "there would be no safety."[26]

Little Failure does indeed frankly confront difficult material. The memoir, which is "novelistic" in its narrative pacing and generation of suspense, sets readers up for a long-prepared-for climax in which the source of the author's adult panic attacks is uncovered, back on Russian soil, in the disclosure of a traumatic and apparently repressed childhood event. The mystery to be solved is, more broadly, the history behind Shteyngart's conflicts with his parents and his impression of being victimized by their own sense of inadequacy and failure. "*Failurchka,*" or "Little Failure," was the half-kidding nickname Shteyngart received, like Vladimir Girshkin, from his own mother. Much of the memoir tracks the growing rift between Shteyngart and his parents as he leaves childhood, particularly in regard to religion and political ideology: his parents are Republicans, and his father an ardent supporter of Israel. His later stature as a celebrity only exacerbates this schism, for his public statements come to seem like—and, he concedes, were sometimes meant to be—pointed refutations of his parents' cherished beliefs:

> "We are living different lives," my father says, astutely. "And it makes me sad."
>
> It makes me sad, too. But what can be done? I used to be more forthcoming with my father, and, consequently, I used to hate him. Now I know just how much pain I can inflict, and do inflict, with each book I publish that does not extol the State of Israel, with each National Public Radio pronouncement that does not bind me in covenant with his famous God.[27]

Compounding the tension between father and son is the former's sense of having been thwarted in his own vocation:

> "I went to the same musical school in Leningrad as [the famous soprano, Galina Vishnevskaya]. They ruined her voice, and they ruined my voice, too. They made me a bass instead of a baritone."
>
> [My father's complaints are] about him now. About his opera career, the one he gave up to become, like most Soviet Jewish men, a mechanical engineer. It's not about me. I breathe easily. At another recent dinner my father had put his arm around me, his face so close to mine that the whites and grays of his goatee nearly touched the grays of my stubble, and said: "I burn with a black envy [chyornaya zavist'] toward you. I should have been an artist as well."[28]

Shteyngart may have had a very different political identity than his father—who collected videotapes with titles such as "Immigration: Threatening the Bonds of Our Union: Part II: Treachery and Treason in America"[29]—but essential patterns of expression have been passed along to him. His fiction, he has conceded, has emulated both parents' often caustic humor: "This is how they talk. This is how I never learned to talk. Not in Russian. Not in English. The supposedly funny banter with a twist of the knife. That's what I have my novels for."[30]

Another painful divergence between Shteyngart and his parents concerns his sense that the substance of one's family life is more or less fair game for fiction. Shortly after the appearance of his first novel, he is forced to confront the difference between his American comfort with publicity, nurtured in part by his experience of psychoanalysis, and his parents' Old World attachment to privacy:

> It is my father's voice [on the phone]. "Mudak," he says. My mother's howling takes up the rest of the conversation.
>
> The Russian word mudak stems from the ancient term for "testicles," and in a rural sense connotes a castrated piglet. In a modern sense it is perhaps closest to the American "dickhead." In my father's arsenal of words I know that it is the nuclear option, and that's what it feels like when he says it. . . .
>
> Mudak. Added to Snotty and Weakling and Little Failure, this may be the final word to grace the tombstone of our relationship. Because while the hurt is still thrumming in my ear—why can't you be proud of me in my finest moment to date?—I am back on my psychoanalyst's couch trying on the new words I've just taught myself.
>
> I am not a bad son.
>
> Through the howling coming at me from across the East River, I discern the source of my parents' anger, the mudak-inciting pain. A Jewish newspaper has sent a reporter to meet my parents in their natural habitat and

> in her subsequent article has suggested that my parents somewhat resemble the hero's parents in my novel.
>
> "We don't ever want to speak to you again," my mother is shouting at me.[31]

In writing the memoir, Shteyngart confessed, he struggled with the ethics of exposing more family secrets, especially without the partially protective cover of fiction that his novels have provided. His aim was to make sense of his parents' enduring dysfunction, but he was aware of the risk of causing further pain: "What does that feel like for them [to be mocked in their son's fiction]? What does it feel like to pick up a book, or an article in a Jewish newspaper, and not fully understand the subtlety, the irony, the satire of the world depicted therein? What does it feel like to be unable to respond in the language with which that mockery is issued?"[32] Shteyngart's justification for writing unflattering *nonfiction* versions of his parents, he concluded, was to give proper voice to their suffering—"How can I not publicize that pain?"[33]—as he searched for its origins in their Soviet past.

This attempt to redeem past public exposures with new ones suggests another ironic connection with Shteyngart's fiction, for *Little Failure* was written soon after *Super Sad True Love Story,* a novel which explores troubled parent-child relationships and examines the willing surrender of privacy and the self-commodification of intimate memories, which have become routine in an age of fevered and ostensibly therapeutic self-revelation. Shteyngart's efforts to "publicize [his family's] pain" from his position as a celebrity author are necessarily bound up with his own self-promotion and ongoing evolution as a literary commodity. As Sean Redmond noted of the dynamics of celebrity "confessionals," "Stars and celebrities confess—they always have invested in the revelatory mode of self-enunciation—but in the self-reflexive, ubiquitous, highly simulated environment of 24/7 media culture today, they centrally rely on the confessional to authenticate, validate, humanize, resurrect, extend and enrich their star and celebrity identities. Stars and celebrities confess, and in so doing confirm their status as truthful, emotive, experiential beings who—as devotional fans—we can invest in."[34]

Little Failure in fact may be thought of as telling its own super sad true American love story for the twenty-first century: an immigrant mostly fails to find adequate acceptance within his family and the specific heritage it offers to him, and so gradually invents, within the public sphere, a self deserving of love and able to claim it:

> In the year 2000 it is still possible to woo a girl with a book deal. And woo I do. But what's so amazing is how quickly I am wooed back. How soon

> a number of warm and attractive women are keen to walk down the street with me, hand in hand. . . . I'm not stupid when it comes to these matters. I know how little attraction I pose for most women à la carte. And what I realize is that with [this success] . . . I will never have to go home to an empty bed again. From this point forward, I will know love whenever I need to know it.[35]

Essential to Shteyngart's self-invention, the memoir made clear, was his navigation of the complex dynamics of group identity in multicultural New York. He was enrolled in Hebrew school (the Solomon Schecter School of Queens), but his Russian background and rudimentary English alienated him from other students. When he was eight, his parents insisted that he be circumcised, a psychologically and physically painful event fictionalized—and, one rather hopes, greatly exaggerated—in *Absurdistan,* where the eighteen-year-old Misha, at the behest of his father, undergoes the procedure and is horrifically disfigured. Shteyngart recalled his confusion and frustration at not being accepted by his peers in spite of this sacrifice:

> [Coming to America] wasn't all about the money. We came to be Jews, right? Or at least my father did. I didn't really have any feelings on the subject one way or another. And now there has to be simvolizm [symbolism]. And that's why I've been cut so brutally, to be more like the children who hate me so much at school, who hate me more than I will ever be hated for the rest of my life. They hate me because I come from the country our new president will soon declare to be the "Evil Empire," giving rise to the endless category of movies beginning with the word "Red"—Red Dawn, Red Gerbil, Red Hamster. "Commie!" they shout, with a jolly push into a soft Hebrew school wall. "Russki!"
>
> But I got cut down there for you! I want to shout back at them. I left Latin Lenin [a statue in which the famous leader seems to be salsa-dancing] in Moscow Square just to get this circumcision. I'm a Jew like you, and doesn't that matter more than where I was born?[36]

Shteyngart's sense of being a marginal presence within an already-marginalized group deepened after this experience, along with his impression that *Russian*—rather than Jewish or American—was primary among his affiliations.

The prejudices cultivated within that marginality are candidly exposed in *Little Failure.* Shteyngart's parents were terrified of Hispanic and African Americans and perversely proud of their own position in the nation's racial hierarchy:

> There are decent public schools in Queens, but we are scared of blacks. If you put together two Soviet immigrants in Queens or Brooklyn circa 1979, the subject of shvartzes or "the Spanish with their transistor radios" would come up by the third sentence. . . . But listen carefully to those conversations. There's hatred and fear, sure, but just a little down the line, laughter and relief. The happy recognition that, as unemployed and clueless as we are, there is a reservoir of disgust in our new homeland for someone other than ourselves. We are refugees and even Jews, which in the Soviet Union never won you any favors, but we are also something that we never really had the chance to appreciate back home. We are white."[37]

Absorbing the fears of his parents, and eager to align himself with the nation's powerful, the teenage Shteyngart even experimented with a staunch Republicanism and a fiercely pro-Israel stance: "[He] volunteered for George Bush Sr.'s scorched-earth presidential campaign against the hapless Michael Dukakis, laughing along with Bush's racist, hysterical Willie Horton commercials and all they imply about the liberal Massachusetts Greek. Compassion, after all, is a virtue only rich Americans can afford, tolerance the purview of slick Manhattanites who already have everything I want."[38]

This political identity did not last long, and, soon after Bush's victory, Shteyngart dramatically changed course and began, with a growing appreciation for America's rich diversity, to stake out his ideological differences from his parents: "The racism inside me is dying, a difficult, smelly death. Looking down at others is one of the few things that has kept me afloat through the years, the comfort in thinking that entire races are lower than my family, lower than me. But New York City is making it hard. Stuyvesant [his ethnically diverse high school] is making it hard. What's there to say when the smartest boy in school is of Palestinian descent by way of South Africa?"[39]

After enrolling at Oberlin, a prestigious liberal arts institution in the American Midwest that is parodied as Accidental College in *Absurdistan,* Shteyngart discovered the broader cultural cachet of his own ethnic identity—which, as in his fiction, he satirized while nevertheless affirming its underlying, unironic personal significance. Occupying the role of "outsider" here can, he discovered, be leveraged for personal advantage in an academic milieu dominated by liberal fastidiousness:

> I master an Oberlin technique called "As a."
>
> "As a woman, I think . . ." "As a woman of color, I would speculate . . ." "As a woman of no color, I would conjecture . . ." "As a hermaphrodite." "As a bee liberator." "As a beagle in a former life."

> Only what will I say? Whom will I speak for? I raise my hand. "As an immigrant . . ." Pause. All eyes on me. This isn't Stuyvesant; here immigrants are a rare, succulent breed, even if the ones present usually have parents who own half of Lahore. "As an immigrant from the former Soviet Union . . ." So far, so good! Where can I take this? "As an immigrant from a developing country crushed by American imperialism . . ."
>
> As I speak, people, by which I mean girls, are looking at me and nodding. I have shed every last vestige of the Hebrew school nudnik and the Stuyvesant clown.[40]

A major in political science and creative writing, Shteyngart was well positioned to study the imaginative constructions—and social power struggles—that inform group identity formations. The speciousness of at least some of those formations is repeatedly lampooned in his first two novels, which posit "progressive" rhetoric as, at least on some level, a means of easing guilt over material acquisition:

> "But you're wealthy yourself," Harry protested. . . ." You have a chauffeur, a BMW, that nice felt hat."
>
> "But that is my right!" Vladimir bellowed. . . ." Have you not heard of identity politics?" [he] shouted. "Are you daft, man? To be rich in my own milieu, to partake in the economic rebirth of my own part of the world, why, if that's not part of my narrative, what the hell is?"[41]

Shteyngart has suggested that Oberlin ultimately provided a valuable sort of "accidental" education for him—its liberal pedagogy a lesson in banal sentimentalism, its Marxist posturing a reminder of the entrenched American class structure: "The truth is this: The rich will rule even at a place like Oberlin, where their kind is technically forbidden. They will simply invert the power structure to suit their needs."[42]

Though he may have convinced other Oberlin students of his authenticity as a Russian, Shteyngart, in his early attempts to write like one—incorporating family stories as an ethnic "insider"—failed decisively. After his mother read his "earnest homage to [his] uncle Aaron and the labor camps,"[43] she bluntly told him that he had misrepresented essential facts: "I am heartbroken. Oddly enough, the pain feels similar to being called a Red Gerbil in Hebrew school. There, I was ridiculed for being an inauthentic American, and now I am being charged with being an inauthentic Russian. I do not yet understand that this very paradox is the true subject of so-called immigrant fiction."[44] Questions of authenticity are of course prominent in *The Russian Debutante's Handbook* and *Absurdistan,* which exuberantly toy with notions of ethnicity while mocking the peculiar irrationality and insubstantiality of Oberlin-style identity politics. The ethnic caricatures of those novels—especially of Russian gangster-oligarchs—in fact seem deliberately calculated to suggest the fantastical quality of perceptions of the "Other," while also perhaps daring critics to complain about the author's own complicity in stereotyping, for which, he knows, liberal commentators will likely give him the benefit of the doubt, given his insider credentials.

In a 2004 essay called "The New Two-Way Street," Shteyngart emphasized the choice involved in assuming identities in contemporary America: "Today, people like myself, Russians by birth and Americans by education, don't need to choose a single, exclusive identity. Equally at home (and equally homeless) in both cultures, we are global citizens of an increasingly borderless world."[45] Each of Shteyngart's novels explores the allure of multiplicity—the pleasures of being free to invent oneself—along with the sometimes oppressive burden of *having* to choose between identities. As the sociologist Zygmunt Bauman remarked of the existential crises generated by the contemporary availability of shifting identities, "After all, asking 'who you are' makes sense to you only once you believe that you can be someone other than you are; only if you have a choice, and only if it depends on you what you choose; only if you have to do something, that is, for the choice to be 'real' and to hold."[46] For Vladimir Girshkin and Misha Vainberg, guilt and ambivalence haunt "global citizenship," and both seem to yearn for an escape from choice, from the need to wander, a way to feel properly and finally grounded in a single place. Lenny Abramov seeks to escape *any* sort of limiting identity by living forever, though the failure of this ambition suggests a surrender to borders, to the inevitability of having to select a fixed residence for the self.

Identity is always, Shteyngart has suggested in both his novels and his memoir, at least partly a matter of strategic performance and contingent interpretation—a fluid and relentlessly updated "construct," in contemporary parlance, not a "natural" fact. His sense of his Russian ethnicity as both significant and real, and yet also a matter of rhetorical achievement, seems on display in an author profile appearing shortly after the publication of *The Russian Debutante's Handbook*. Daniel Zalewski interviewed Shteyngart at his parents' home—in part, it seems, to provide a sense of the authentic ethnic ground from which this new Russian author had bloomed—and summarized his self-description in terms that suggest both the sincerity of his avowal of "Otherness" and his canny strategizing in marketing that identity in the most saleable form possible. The result is a sort of sophisticated revision of the author's early, debutant pitch to his classmates at Oberlin: "Just as Nabokov never got over the agony of exile, Shteyngart has never been able to embrace fully his identity as an

American. He has described himself as a 'global writer' who is, first and foremost, a Russian."[47]

Shteyngart's representation of his Jewish affiliation in *Little Failure* contains its own complexities. While the memoir offers itself primarily as a record of his personal acculturation, he nevertheless frames his family's attitudes—which he insistently characterizes as paranoid, racist, and more or less indifferent to the particularities of Jewish religious life—as broadly representative of those of other Soviet Jews arriving in America during roughly the same period. Though for the most part he has been received very positively by Jewish American literary critics—*The Russian Debutante's Handbook,* for instance, won the National Jewish Book Award for fiction, and Shteyngart is regularly invited to give readings by Jewish groups—his description of Soviet Jews in his memoir has been controversial. In response to Shteyngart's rather enigmatic claims about his family's group identity—"We Soviet Jews were simply invited to the wrong party. And then we were too frightened to leave. Because we didn't know who we were. In this book, I'm trying to say who we were"[48]—Marat Grinberg vigorously affirmed that it "is unquestionable that Jews who left the Soviet Union in the 1970s and 1980s knew exactly what they were leaving and where they were going. And they got there."[49] Shteyngart is grossly unfair, argued Grinberg, in suggesting that his family's dysfunction is typical, in equating Jewish Republicanism and racism, and in positing Russian culture as much more significant than Judaism to the Soviet-Jewish diaspora. After describing some of the ways in which "the traces of Jewish memory functioned in the Soviet context,"[50] Grinberg concluded by positing Shteyngart as something like an ethnic traitor: "And so the infamous Soviet project of hollowing out Jewishness, which should have died with the death of the Communist regime, has now entered American literature—through the work of Gary Shteyngart."[51]

Without doubt Shteyngart's depiction of Jews in both his fiction and nonfiction has been acerbic and provocative. The three novels give us various representatives of the sort of hollowed-out Jewishness—that is, a Jewishness emptied of Judaism and animated by racialized phobias—critiqued by Grinberg. Vladimir Girshkin's mother in *The Russian Debutante's Handbook* is marked by "a peerless Russian racism" and tipsily prays to Jesus, since the Jewish God "hasn't been helping much lately,"[52] while his father worships Pushkin and Lermontov rather than the Torah. Boris Vainberg in *Absurdistan* functions as a caricature of a Jewish conservative and harbors versions of the prejudices that Shteyngart located in his own parents: "Papa's racism was a thing to behold, impenetrable, subsuming, all-encompassing, an epic poem."[53] Misha unleashes a startling anti-Semitic rant in the novel after encountering a Hasidic man eating a kosher meal on a plane and is the most enthusiastic celebrant of Russian high culture—he likens himself to Oblomov and Prince Myshkin—in all of Shteyngart's fiction. In *Super Sad True Love Story,* the Abramovs are, like Vladimir's parents, seemingly close, if parodic, analogues to Shteyngart's own: they possess an "inbred Soviet Jewish conservatism" and spend much of their time watching right-wing propaganda such as "FoxLiberty-Prime and Fox-Liberty-Ultra"[54] on television. Lenny's father blithely recommends, moreover, that "SecurityState Israel . . . use the nuclear option against the Arabs and the Persians."[55] In his youth, Lenny recalls, the family used to visit impoverished areas of New York City in order to reaffirm—in a fashion consonant with the attitudes typical of the Russian American Jews that Shteyngart described in *Little Failure*—a sense of their economic, and racial, superiority:

> [My] parents used to drive me around in their rusted Chevrolet Malibu Classic to neighborhoods poorer than our own, so that we could both laugh at the funny ragtag brown people scurrying about in their sandals and pick up important lessons about what failure could mean in America. It was after my parents told Mrs. Fine about our little slumming forays into Corona and the safer parts of Bed-Stuy that the rupture between her and my family truly began. I remember my parents looking up "cruel" in the English-Russian dictionary, shocked that our American mama could possibly think that of us.[56]

And, like the Girshkins, the Abramovs seem to prefer Russian culture, if not Russia itself, to Judaism: "Although [they] never had a good word to say about HolyPetroRussia, the hallways were hung with framed sepia-toned postcards of Red Square and the Kremlin; the snow-dusted equestrian statue of Prince Yuri Dolgorukiy, founder of Moscow . . . and the gothic Stalin-era skyscraper of prestigious Moscow State University."[57] In *Little Failure,* Shteyngart's descriptions of Jewish Americans who helped his family acculturate are often sardonic, as in this description of his father being "discovered" by a group of zealous true believers: "when they realize he's one of the mythical Russian Jews they've heard about on TV, one of their long-lost coreligionists, they shower him with unadulterated love. One of them, a follower of the ultranationalist Rabbi Kahane, gives him ten American dollars. It is the Sabbath and handling money is verboten, but making sure a Jew has enough to eat takes precedence."[58] Kahane is, Shteyngart has noted, the leader of Kach, a "soon-to-be-outlawed organization in Israel—driving the Arabs into the sea a central plank of their platform,"[59] and he adds in a footnote that "Eventually the State Department will add Kach to its list of foreign terrorist organizations, and the rabbi himself will be assassinated in New York in 1990."[60]

Questioned in a 2014 interview with Renee Ghert-Zand of the *Times of Israel* about how he might separate his sense of being a Russian and being a Jew, Shteyngart characteristically suggested the interdependence of the two identities, while bending the Jewish element toward the Russian: "In America so many Jews are of Russian, Ukrainian or Belorussian extraction, maybe three generations down the line. That's why you get so much of this Seinfeld-ian kind of humor. It's a very distressed kind of humor from the edge of the grave. I'm just closer to the source of it than many American Jews whose families have been here for a while."[61] In Shteyngart's representation of his family, and of Russian American Jews more generally, Jewishness is finally a *cultural* rather than a religious identity—one that recognizes a fundamental affiliation with Russian achievements even as it mourns a history of persecution by the Russian gentile majority.

This stance was in fact typical among Soviet Jews, whose religion was vigorously suppressed as part of official state policy. The Jewish turn to Russian traditions forms what Yuri Slezkine has called "the Pushkin faith," a strategy by which a persecuted minority claimed its own stake in "Russianness" through a knowledge of that culture's elite products: "As elsewhere in Europe, the Jewish success in Russian business, the professions, and the arts (often in that order within one family), was accompanied by a mastery of the national high culture and an eager conversion to the Pushkin faith."[62] In *Little Failure,* Shteyngart wrote of his parents' respect for Russian traditions in the abstract, compared to their contempt for the actual conditions of Russia itself, again paralleling the Girshkins in *The Russian Debutante's Handbook:* "In the decade since we've emigrated, my parents have never said one good word about the country, other than to praise its many bearded writers and creamy Eskimo ice cream."[63] His family practices, Shteyngart implied, a form of the Pushkin faith, their altar the "glass-and-mahogany bookcase that is the focal point of every Russian household,"[64] which "contains the collected works of Anton Chekhov in eight dark blue volumes with the author's seagull-like signature across every volume's cover, and most of the collected works of Tolstoy, Dostoyevsky, and Pushkin. In front of the Russian greats stands a siddur (the Jewish daily prayer book), enclosed in a plastic case and coated with fake silver and fake emeralds. It is written in a language none of us understands, but it is so holy that it blocks out the Pushkin that my parents have all but committed to memory."[65] It is Russian texts his parents had absorbed and continued to worship, and though the siddur was respected as a holy item, it stands, Shteyngart implied, as a kind of empty, even *poshlost* symbol of an outgrown faith.

Early in *Little Failure,* Shteyngart described a panic attack he experienced in 1996, after leafing through a coffee-table book featuring the architecture of St. Petersburg:

> And here's what I was looking at as my brain rolled around its stony cavity: a church. The Chesme Church on Lensovet (Leningrad Soviet) Street in the Moskovsky District of the city formerly known as Leningrad. Eight years later I would describe it . . . for a Travel + Leisure article, . . . [but] in 1996 I did not have the wherewithal to spin clever prose. I had not yet undergone twelve years of four-times-a-week psychoanalysis that would make of me a sleekly rational animal, able to quantify, catalog, and retreat casually from most sources of pain, save one. I beheld the tiny scale of the church; the photographer had framed it between two trees, and there was a stretch of potholed asphalt in front of its diminutive entrance. It looked vaguely like a child overdressed for a ceremony. Like a little red-faced, tiny-bellied failure. It looked like how I felt.[66]

The psychological sources of the attack were revealed in the memoir's final chapter, as Shteyngart returned to Lensovet Street in 2011 with his parents:

> There are cheap lace curtains in the windows of the apartment blocks. The hotel Mir, which I've once unfairly described as the "the worst hotel in the world," sits on one side of the street. We step over crooked train lines and unkempt vegetation. A soot-covered truck passes by. My father begins to speak rapidly, as if he has been building up the courage to do so.
>
> "As I was telling you, little son, one day when we were walking down this street after launching our [toy] helicopter by the church, we were going back to our house and you started to behave rascally [ty nachal shalit']. You were still trying to launch the helicopter on the street and there were so many people around. I told you once, twice, you didn't listen, then I swung my fist and you got it in the nose. And the blood began to flow."[67]

This single abusive act is uncovered as a kind of primal scene in the drama of Shteyngart's distressed relationship with his parents. In traveling back to his childhood home and confronting the origins of his own—and their—pathologies, he contended, he had begun to exorcise a haunting past.

The conclusion of the memoir brings the reader to a village outside of modern-day St. Petersburg, where Shteyngart and his parents visited his paternal grandfather's grave, located within a memorial to fallen soldiers of World War II. His reckoning of the significance of this event is characteristic in emphasizing the importance of his Russian heritage: "It is not an exaggeration to say that those of us who are Russian, or Russian American, or Russian anything, are the offspring of these [WW II] battles" (346). Reading the mourner's kaddish over his grandfather's tomb, he transferred the Hebrew words into the dual contexts which have primarily defined him: "I can read the prayer, but I cannot understand it. The words coming out of my mouth are gibberish to me. And they can only be gibberish to my father's ear as well. . . . I chant the gibberish backwards and forwards, tripping over the words, mangling them, making them sound more Russian, more American, more holy" (348).

The memoir thus culminates in a scene of at least provisional familial healing and integration. As Shteyngart affirmed of his dedication to psychoanalysis, the sharing of suffering, the opening up of one's pain to others, can liberate private unrealities into the sanitizing public air: "Four times a week, I have a lunch date with reality. I talk, [my psychoanalyst] listens. . . . Reality. I'm learning to separate the real from the not. As soon as I say something out loud, as soon as I publicize it into the afghan-carpeted Park Avenue air, I realize it is not true. Or: it doesn't have to be true."[68] *Little Failure* is, in a characteristic half-irony, dedicated to Shteyngart's parents as well as his psychoanalyst. If traditional religiosity has indeed been hollowed out in the author's rendering of his experience, it is seemingly replaced by new therapeutic rituals with their own sacred aura: a redemptive public baring of trauma and the confession of sins, leading to revelation.[69]

CHAPTER 6

Shteyngart and American Literary Celebrity

A cursory search on YouTube produces a flood of Shteyngart-related offerings, covering not only the well-known book trailers, but interviews, profiles, and readings conducted across a staggering range of venues. Since the publication of *The Russian Debutante's Handbook* in 2002, Shteyngart has cultivated a celebrity status shared by few contemporary American authors. He is now not just a beloved and bestselling novelist, memoirist, and travel writer, but also a recognizable public figure known for specific traits: above all, a humor, at turns zany and mordant, centered on his persona as an endearingly bumbling Russian immigrant. The construction of this persona intriguingly illustrates some of the mechanics of contemporary self-making, along with essential assumptions about the provisional, always contested nature of identity we encounter in Shteyngart's fiction.

In an article published in the *Guardian* in the spring of 2015, Kate Gwynne included Shteyngart in her profile of ten contemporary authors particularly skilled at social media who were "using the etherland as a canvas for experimentation and play, . . . [having] moved their storytelling, wit and insight from page to pixel, winning fans and readers in the process."[1] Gwynne noted that Shteyngart's posting of pictures of his dachshund on social networking sites took advantage of a "rise in oxytocin levels"[2] produced by looking at cute images, and she praised him for his skills as an entertainer: "When Shteyngart promotes his latest books, he does so palatably. Most book trailers are deadly dull—Shteyngart's showcase the self-deprecating author up to his usual antics, and often include ridiculous cameos, such as James Franco in a pink dressing gown. Humour is a lifesaver for those invariable moments when an author has to toot their own horn."[3]

Predictably, Shteyngart's high visibility has prompted opposing responses from those who prefer that literary authors maintain a greater distance, or at least the pretense of it, from the marketplace. Soon after Gwynne's article appeared, Katy Waldman published a rebuttal in *Slate*—"It's Time to Stop Praising Authors for 'Being Good at the Internet'"—which targeted Shteyngart in particular. Waldman questioned Gwynne's enthusiasm for authors' cultivation of an online presence and ironically pointed to another American author as the current master of the media:

> [Interacting] with the people you want to buy your books isn't in itself an act of inspired imagination, especially when it involves dispatches as random (yet predictably treacly) as dachshund snaps. I'd argue that what really makes an author good at the internet is the same thing that wins any paperbound plotter legions of adoring fans: the element of surprise. And by this metric, the most brilliant internet practitioner in the literary world is Jonathan Franzen . . . [whose] emphatic absence from social media earns him tons of relevant publicity, cementing his image as the curmudgeonly champion of an old-school world of letters.[4]

Of course, Franzen's absence has not been *that* emphatic, since he has appeared in one of Shteyngart's own book trailers.[5]

Such debates about the seemliness of some modes of marketing suggest the importance in the contemporary literary world of extra-literary public performances that act as supplements to, or even replacements for, the actual writing that has ostensibly brought authors their renown. There is nothing radically new, of course, about vigorous self-promotion in the history of literary publishing, and the American canon includes many figures who were extraordinary, and to varying degrees even controversial, commercial innovators. In fact the marketing efforts of Benjamin Franklin, Walt Whitman, and Mark Twain—a trio whose authorial personalities loom large over their literary works—offer intriguing analogues to Shteyngart's own success as a literary celebrity.

In the eighteenth century, Franklin prospered as a publisher and author through his mastery of a variety of advertising techniques, including the penning of pseudonymous articles calculated to meet the demands of contemporary readers. His creative entrance into the literary marketplace began at the age of fifteen, when he wrote a series of letters to his brother's paper in the voice of a middle-aged widow named Mrs. Silence Dogood. Franklin's later writing presented a version of himself as the ultimate self-made man—his narrative of fabulous achievement codified in his *Autobiography* (1793)—which endures today as a national archetype. It is likely that only a relatively small proportion of contemporary Americans have actually read Franklin's autobiography, but surely the vast majority could identify his image (immortalized on the hundred dollar bill), his assumed personality (a mythic mix of intelligence, creativity, diligence, frugality, and good humor), and his ultimate import (an icon for the American Dream). Well aware of his own public image, Franklin crafted distinct personae for himself at home and abroad, dressing up when he went to France, for instance, in a costume meant to evoke an American frontiersman. As his biographer Walter Isaacson related of the role-playing, both shrewd and playful, involved here:

> [Franklin's] new rustic look was partly a pose, the clever creation of America's first great image-maker and public relations master. He wore his soft marten fur cap, the one he had picked up on his trip to Canada, during most of his social outings, including when he was received at the famous literary salon of Madame du Deffand shortly after his arrival, and it became a feature in the portraits and medallions of him. The cap, like that worn by Rousseau, served as his badge of homespun purity and New World virtue, just as his ever-present spectacles (also featured in portraits) became an emblem of wisdom. It helped him play the part that Paris imagined for him: that of the noble frontier philosopher and simple backwoods sage—even though he had lived most of his life on Market Street and Craven Street.[6]

Shteyngart's public persona has affinities with Franklin's not only in its arch role-playing, which also sometimes includes costumes, as in the famous author photo from *The Russian Debutante's Handbook,* but in its association with the rhetoric of American self-making. Part of his appeal in the contemporary marketplace no doubt has to do with his alignment with an enduringly alluring narrative of national success, for Shteyngart's story is in an important sense a retelling of the great American myth: a plucky ascent from nothing or very little to great professional and material achievement, a marvelous self-transformation undertaken in defiance of limiting origins and made possible by committed individual effort. As the publisher's blurb for Shteyngart's memoir puts it, "*Little Failure* is the all too true story of an immigrant family betting its future on America, as told by a lifelong misfit who finally finds a place for himself in the world through books and words."[7] Though Shteyngart himself has tended to emphasize his Russian affiliation, and his memoir itself culminates in a revelatory return to his childhood home, his success story is definitively pitched as an American one, a confirmation of the unique conditions available in the land of opportunity.

Shteyngart certainly seems Franklinian too in his thorough understanding of the mechanics of the publishing industry and in his assiduous manipulations of them. Since the publication of *Super Sad True Love Story* in 2010, he has become known in particular for his extraordinarily prolific blurbing. A recent reviewer of a Croatian American novel remarked on the predictability of the author's stamp of approval on new literary titles: "[This] debut arrives flanked by the kind of marketing campaign that makes the monster trucks of *Mad Max: Fury Road* look like Tonka toys. It comes with the requisite admiring blurb by Gary Shteyngart and US publisher Little, Brown's announcement that the book is one of their lead fiction titles for 2015."[8] By current count Shteyngart has blurbed approximately two hundred books with no sign of letting up despite an open letter to the *New Yorker* in the spring of 2014 in which he professed a new discrimination in choosing deserving titles.[9] In 2013 Edward Champion produced a brief documentary—*Shteyngart Blurbs*—that comically examines New York blurbing culture and Shteyngart's place within it.[10] The fifteen-minute video features a number of the recipients of the author's praise, who express their gratitude, amid comic asides, at the endorsement of a celebrity author. Interviewed at his home, apparently while in the middle of blurbing multiple books, Shteyngart explained his intention to promote worthy writing that might otherwise go unnoticed, while confessing with apparent seriousness that he does not actually finish reading many of the books he blurbs: "I'm trying to get people to read good serious literary fiction, or funny literary fiction, and no hyperbole can be hyperbolic enough, because very few people want to read this stuff. I read some of them through completely . . . and some books you just read for as much as you have time to read and then you get a general sense that it's something that you would enjoy reading to the end if you had the time."[11]

The comic gusto of Shteyngart's blurbing seems similar, at least in terms of its knowing playfulness, to his treatment of ethnic caricatures in his fiction. The blurbs both traffic in and parody stereotypes and seem intended partly as a source of imaginative fun, offering a means of indulging in lively distortions, spoofing authors' yearning for praise, and mocking the willingness of marketers to say anything in order to increase sales. And yet they also often convey a certain seriousness—a genuine appeal to pay attention to something important going on beyond the playfulness whether it happens to reside in the book being blurbed or not. Shteyngart's blurbs typically imply a kind of lighthearted, transparent hyperbole—"When a new Ken Kalfus novel appears I stop eating, drinking, shaving, and breathing until I finish it. *Equilateral* is one of his smartest and most ambitious books yet. It left me thinking and wondering well past my bedtime"—but sometimes bend toward what can seem like at least half-serious affirmations. His blurb of Sara Nović's *Girl at War,* for instance, called the novel "an unforgettable portrait of how war forever changes the life of the individual," and Kiran Desai's *The Inheritance of Loss* received even higher praise: "If God is in the details, Ms. Desai has written a holy book. Page after page, from Harlem to the Himalayas, she captures the terror and exhilaration of being alive in the world."[12] The Nović blurb combines banality and vagueness ("how war forever changes the life of the individual") with an apparently genuine promise of something more ("an unforgettable portrait"). The Desai blurb opens with an ironic compliment ("a holy book"), which only those familiar with Shteyngart's vocal atheism would be likely to appreciate fully, then proffers, after the somewhat flippant—but not *too* flippant—alliteration of "Page after page, from Harlem to the Himalayas," an enormous compliment ("she captures the terror and exhilaration of being alive in the world") even if once again it is also somewhat banal and vague.

These blurbs can be read as short meta-narratives in themselves that posit an elite audience of insiders. Their ironic implications certainly become complex: "Shteyngart," it seems, typically both does and does not really mean what is written above his name, and the blurbs come to function as long-running inside jokes, slowly compounded with more levels of awareness between blurber and ideal audience, with the latter tending in the end to be a small group of fellow authors, fellow New Yorkers, who might blurb and be blurbed themselves. And if the joke is lost on some book purchasers who somehow trust the endorser's words and are led to sample something that might not otherwise have captured their attention, all the better for the commercial success of the book trade. Franklin might well have been delighted by this kind of whimsical mischief, for he loved literary hoaxes and is said to have been denied authorship of the Declaration of Independence because his colleagues feared he would hide indecorous puns in it. He would surely have appreciated the canniness of having one's name appear on the covers of numerous books by other writers, for such visibility contributes to an impression of the author's centrality to the current literary marketplace and the commodities circulating there. Moreover, general readers who may not understand the layered ironies of the blurbs may still find themselves intrigued by their mysterious textual play—and curious enough to explore Shteyngart's own writing further. The potentially deceptive quality of Shteyngart's blurbing might well have struck Vladimir Nabokov, however, as an example of one of the major vices—*poshlost*—satirized in both their fiction: "*Poshlust,*[13] it should be repeated, is especially vigorous and vicious when the sham is *not* obvious and when the values it mimics are considered, rightly or wrongly, to belong to the very highest level of art, thought or emotion. It is those books that are so *poshlustily* reviewed in the literary supplement of daily papers—the best sellers, the 'stirring, profound and beautiful' novels; it is these 'elevated and powerful' books that contain and distil the very essence of *poshlust*."[14]

Twain's experience with self-promotion also forms an illuminating analogue to Shteyngart's. As Joe Moran explained, market conditions in the mid- to late nineteenth century—and especially the prevalence of unauthorized reproductions of authors' works, from which they received no income—pushed Twain and other authors to commodify themselves in pioneering ways:

> A key element in the popularization of the lecture circuit was the promotional power of the press. . . . In lieu of a healthy market for books, authors naturally looked to this thriving print culture for publication and publicity. Apart from the fact that authors wrote for these magazines and newspapers, the latter also reported on the lectures, or sometimes reprinted the speeches in their entirety, accompanying them with illustrations or cartoon caricatures of the speaker, helping to turn the circuit into one frequented by recognized 'names.' One British journalist calculated in 1878 that Twain's speeches were 'probably read by a larger number of men and women in America than any public document, the President's message not excepted.' Twain's lecture tours, as well as being lavishly and expensively advertised in themselves, employed his frequent press interviews as free advance publicity, in the same way that the main purpose of a contemporary celebrity interview is often to 'plug' a book or film.[15]

Twain helped drive sales of his works by presenting himself as an entertaining comic character—instantly recognizable in white suit and wild hair—which he portrayed in interviews and readings across the country. The name attached to that character—Mark Twain—was itself invented by the man who performed it, Samuel Langhorne Clemens.[16] His lecture tours introduced him as a folksy purveyor of profound home truths: his satirical tales would skewer American hypocrisy, and human frailties generally, but in an exceptionally agreeable way, mixing high- and low-brow modes, light entertainment and more serious literary aspiration. As Justin Kaplan observed, Twain was "always his own biographer," and "the central drama of his mature literary life was his discovery of the usable past."[17] An implicit promise of authenticity was offered in his delivery of that past, tied to the assumption that Twain was speaking from rich personal experience, having seen the country firsthand over a lifetime of rollicking adventures and keen-eyed observation. Moreover, as Loren Glass noted, his verbal felicity contributed to the impression that he was himself quite close to the characters he conjured in public performances: "As a writer who got his start on the lecture circuit and whose specific method of literary realism relied heavily on the accurate transcription of spoken vernacular, Twain himself established the critical habit of authenticating his works through their imagined proximity to his own spoken voice."[18] In other words, what one heard on stage was not simply staged, one was given to understand, but a performance with some tangible bond to the real.

Twenty-first-century authors face their own crises of copyright infringement, along with a striking decline in readership—and thus in the means to make a living from writing alone. In turning to slickly produced book trailers and other creative means of self-promotion, Shteyngart responded in a way that is uncannily reminiscent of Twain's approach. As Shteyngart told an interviewer in 2014, "The bottom line is that people don't want to read that many books, especially younger people. It's statistically shown that there's a huge decline in readership, so you have got to make a movie before you can sell a book. The trailers aren't really about the book that much. They're just a way to get the reader to think, 'Oh, maybe this guy has got an entertaining way of telling stories.' But you've got to do them."[19] Shteyngart's authorial persona resembles Twain's too, for beneath the ironic posturing it involves a similar mix of satire, clowning, and implicit pledges of authentic reportage. Both authors win their audiences by trading on their status as cultural authorities who provide entertaining access to a restricted form of knowledge. For Shteyngart the central source of that authority is his claim to Russianness, just as Twain's was his experience traveling and living across the United States. The focus of his writing—Russian or Russian American protagonists whose life experiences often run teasingly close to the author's—and his self-presentation in interviews position him, if sometimes ironically, but always with an underlying earnestness, as a spokesman for a particular kind of ethnic identity. He has been enthusiastically received in the United States as a "Russian writer," with reviewers frequently comparing him to a series of canonical Russians whose names are often cited in his own writing.

In interviews Shteyngart often comes across as a kind of native informant, as he comments—while alternating between flippant and serious tones—on themes ostensibly essential to Russian identity. Troy Patterson, writing in Slate, provided a representative sketch of this persona in an essay titled "Three Days of Vodka with Gary Shteyngart":

> The novelist Gary Shteyngart rolls down a wet West 52nd Street and swings into a brashly lacquered piano bar called the Russian Vodka Room. . . . The job tonight is to help me explain to myself and everyone exactly what vodka is. . . . The vodka arrives. He pours it but does not drink. "We're

> gonna wait for some toasts." The booze cannot go into his mouth until a proper salute has flowed from his heart—and the drinks cannot go down the hatch until the barman puts out our food, our *zakuski:* "that which you follow the vodka with." The most important part of Russian drinking is Russian eating. A *zakuska* is a sine qua non, with an exception allowed for very tough economic times, when it's acceptable to chase the vodka with a sniff of your own overcoat.
>
> While we wait, we talk about politics, about the totally insane role vodka has played in Russian history. Stalin used it as a truth serum and a torture device. Gorbachev assured himself the displeasure of the people by undertaking a temperance campaign as his first official act. Peter the Great really liked to party. . . . Gary thinks that Dan Savage's boycott of Russian vodka (on the grounds of Putin's anti-gay measures) is a nice symbolic gesture that won't change a thing: "If you could boycott natural gas, now *that* would be something."[20]

Like Twain, Shteyngart's authorial persona is amusing and amiably "democratic" in its emphasis on common pleasures, and yet it also makes claims to a special status, an expertise in the field of an at least somewhat exotic kind of lived experience. Through the author, the performance suggests, one hears the real Russia speaking, and one comes to share an insider's privileged perspective.

Part of the comic dynamic of Shteyngart's assumption of Russianness derives, however, from his ironizing of his own claims to ethnic authenticity, a tactic that reaches its apogee in *Absurdistan,* where he creates an alter ego, "Jerry Shteynfarb," who epitomizes the cynical promotion of oneself as an ethnic brand. Adrian Wanner, in a cogent analysis of Shteyngart's slippery self-positioning, pointed to the author photograph used for *The Russian Debutante's Handbook,* in which he appears "dressed in an unstylish coat and ill-matching woolen hat holding a bear cub on a leash, thus conjuring up all the customary clichés of the 'stinky Russian bear,' the awkward, clumsily dressed immigrant from Eastern Europe, and the Jewish schlemiel."[21] The effect here, as in other send-ups of his own Russianness, such as the buffoonish persona he takes on in his book trailers, is to thwart any potential complaints about the legitimacy of his ethnic identity by implying, with good-natured boldness, that in the end identities are products of invention and persuasion. Shteyngart thus places himself both within and outside the game of ethnic marketing: "Shteyngart's self-ironic performance of identity allows him to have his cake and eat it too: he can partake in the currently profitable 'Russian brand' and at the same time satirize writers who use their real or fake ethnic credentials to increase their sale[s] figures."[22]

Wanner went further in suggesting a certain canny manipulation of contemporary political sensibilities in Shteyngart's claims to Russianness.

> There is a logical connection between Shteyngart's self-representation as a "Russian first and foremost" and his tendency to depict post-Soviet Russia as a marginalized and colonized space. This characterization allows him to claim the cherished status of the materially deprived outsider and underdog (which being a Jew does not confer anymore in the United States). In particular, Shteyngart's affinity for African-American culture seems to stem from his wish to be associated with a "hyphenated" ethnic subculture rather than with the American mainstream. This becomes evident in the parallels that he draws between Russians and African-Americans.[23]

Those "parallels" are most explicit in *Absurdistan,* where the narrator's girlfriend, Rouenna Sales, bluntly notes a connection between Russians and African Americans during a visit to St. Petersburg.

> "You are calling me *sister*?" Lyuba whispered, her sweet Russian soul atremble. She put down her fishing line and spread open her arms. "Then I will be your sister, too, Rouennachka!"
>
> "It's just an African-American expression," I told her.
>
> "It sure is," Rouenna said, coming over to give Lyuba a hug, which the temperate girl tearfully reciprocated. "'Cause, as far as I can tell, all of you Russians are just a bunch of niggaz."[24]

This alignment of Russians and African Americans may seem, as Wanner suggested, like part of an extratextual, and perhaps unbecoming, special pleading on Shteyngart's part, though of course it is set within a novel that unrelentingly mocks suspect claims to marginality, including those made by the privileged narrator, who cartoonishly fetishizes African American culture and has taken on the hip-hop nickname "Snack Daddy." Characteristically Shteyngart both has posited an affiliation with African Americans in constructing his own identity as a "marginal Russian" author (that he would "eat" his cake, according to Wanner's idiom) and satirically negated the affiliation as he aligned it with other projects of ostensible "identity theft" (continuing to "have" it, too).

The politics and commercial reception of Shteyngart's construction of Jewish identity are equally complex. His writing often satirizes orthodox Judaism and furnishes numerous unflattering representations of Jews. For instance, *Absurdistan* includes a provocative depiction of the narrator's sponsorship of a Holocaust Museum, which, it is implied, is to act as a means for comfortable and unthreatened Jews to leverage historical guilt. Shteyngart's works have, however, remained popular among Jewish readers, even winning several prominent awards for Jewish authors, and they have been celebrated as part of a strong, and distinctive, category of contemporary ethnic American fiction. One possible reason for this popularity, as Adam Rovner suggested in relation to *The Russian Debutante's Handbook,* may be that Shteyngart's work feeds a nostalgia for cultural difference among Jews. By emphasizing that Jews remain fundamentally unassimilated and even unassimilable in the United States, Shteyngart has proffered a satisfying sense of cultural integrity—and has positioned himself as the spokesman for that integrity—through "an unmediated version of Jewish difference."[25] Such claims to distinctiveness have, as Rovner noted, an obvious commercial appeal in the contemporary literary marketplace: "On college and university syllabi, multiculturalism has taken the welcome form of narratives that emphasize disempowerment and gender-based, sexual, racial, linguistic, and socioeconomic marginality. Proposing and disseminating notions of Jewish difference has become a means of assimilating into an America that celebrates heterogeneity and glamorizes the ethnic chic."[26]

Shifting identifications and the imaginative "containment" of multitudes, no matter the contradictions, are hallmarks of the poetry of Walt Whitman, who is repeatedly invoked in Shteyngart's works. Both authors are vocal celebrants of New York's cultural diversity, and Shteyngart in fact dubbed Whitman his "future best friend"[27] during the recollection of a childhood memory in *Little Failure.* In *Absurdistan,* Misha shares a Whitmanic fantasy of flying over Manhattan and taking in its multitudes while listening to John Lennon's "Imagine": "I *imagined* flying over the city in a helicopter, absorbing its many architectural flourishes and dramatic natural features, but the chopper just kept flying in a northwesterly direction until it reached the southern tip of Manhattan island, spread its helicopter shadow over the asphalt conglomeration of downtown and midtown, then streaked past the gables and dormers of the Dakota Apartments on New York's Central Park, where Mr. Lennon once lived and died."[28] A Whitman poem is also invoked by Joshie Goldman in *Super Sad True Love Story*—"there's a great line by an old poet Walt Whitman: 'Are you the New person drawn to Me?'"[29]—and by Shteyngart himself in an article for the *New Yorker* in which he reported on his experiences using Google Glass: "I hear that in San Francisco, where these devices are far more in evidence, the term 'Glassholes' is already current, but in New York I am a conquering hero. I pass by fascinated faces looking intently into my own unremarkable *punim* [Yiddish, "face"], as I update Walt Whitman's poem—'Are You the New Dork Drawn Toward Me?'"[30]

These tributes—though ironized in their suggestion of inert, narcissistic versions of visionary containment—point to a broader affiliation in authorial personae. If Franklin seems like the grand archetype of Shteyngart's appeals to American dreaming, and Twain of his comic but nevertheless earnest role-playing as a native informant, Whitman provides an analogue for the charismatic soul baring that forms an essential part of Shteyngart's self-promotion. In *Walt Whitman and the Culture of American Celebrity* (2006), David Haven Blake analyzed the nineteenth-century poet's "remarkable merger of poetry and publicity"[31] as he adapted newly emerging advertising techniques—such as the use of photographs—in celebrating himself. Though it took decades before Whitman achieved much in the way of a wide public response to his writing, he sought celebrity by offering his personality as a commodity, entering a marketplace that, by the middle of the nineteenth century, was becoming increasingly crowded with others vying for renown. As Blake explained, Whitman was himself an ardent consumer of "personalities" in this new environment of celebrity exposure:

> Publications in Europe and the United States included information about what leading figures "looked like, what they wore, what they ate, and what they said." The inclusion—and, indeed, featuring—of such information suggests a growing tendency to elevate persona over content, to value the performance, background, or inner life of individuals alongside their substantive accomplishments. From different pen and pencil marks, we know that Whitman was quite typical of antebellum readers in his attraction to personality and anecdote. When he read an 1849 essay in the *North British Review,* for example, he regularly marked passages about Chaucer's life and career while noting very little about the verse. He marked a footnote describing the poet's physical characteristics with particular vigor, writing in the margins "Person."[32]

Keenly aware of what attracted *him* in the personalities of celebrity authors, Whitman set out to construct and publicly bare an irresistible version of himself. Readers of *Leaves of Grass* —and above all of the poem which became "Song of Myself"—encounter the intimate confessions of "Walt Whitman, a kosmos, of Manhattan the son, / Turbulent, fleshy, sensual, eating, drinking and breeding."[33] Privacy, it is promised here, will yield to full exposure: to read the work will be to know the author's deepest, dramatic truths.

In a commercial environment much more densely populated with public figures than the one Whitman knew, Shteyngart similarly engages in a rhetoric of intimacy and personal revelation. His novels invite autobiographical readings and tease readers with the sense that they are sharing in the author's actual experiences as well as his inner life. In interviews about his novels, Shteyngart typically has emphasized the parallels between the facts of his life and their translations into fiction, thus implicitly promising that, no matter how outrageous their comic mode, the latter still offer credible revelations of the author's personality. In fact a challenge he faced in his memoir was to convince readers that more was left to reveal, that his fiction had not already shared all the personal stories worth telling. As he related in one of the passages most often quoted by reviewers of the memoir: "On so many occasions in my novels I have approached a certain truth only to turn away from it, only to point my finger and laugh at it and then scurry back to safety. In this book, I promised myself I would not point the finger. My laughter would be intermittent. There would be no safety."[34] That is, if the personal goods have not yet been delivered in the fiction, they will be now.

A long-term psychoanalytic patient, Shteyngart brings an overtly confessional approach to all his writing, while suggesting—again like Whitman, though in a much less grandiose form—the profound imbrication of individual and national histories.[35] In an article for *Travel + Leisure,* for instance, he personalized his assessment of "The New Moscow" with a reflection on the wider therapeutic value of travel itself.

> We travel to find out where we come from and who we are, those little shards of identity that fall out of a stall in a Hong Kong market or float up with Proustian clarity from the bottom of a Hungarian goulash. But for those of us from somewhere else, it's not just clarity we seek; a part of us wants to rewrite history. *If Russia can become a normal country, then maybe my past can be normalized, too*. It's a hopeless and romantic task, but then again you don't get to choose where you're born, which language your parents speak to you when they soothe your first cut with iodine and Mishka the Clumsy Bear chocolate candy, and which wooden ladle they use to stir your summer borscht.[36]

Much less optimistic than Whitman about both individuals and nations, Shteyngart nevertheless has offered his own experiences as an instructive model, conjuring an exotic allure around highly personal inner and outer voyages that, he has implied, others might replicate on their own.

Particularly since his hiring at Columbia as a professor in 2007, at which point he was already the author of two best-selling novels, Shteyngart's profiles in various media have also emphasized not just where he came from as an upstart "immigrant author," but his lifestyle as a successful, renowned literary figure. The allure of authorial celebrity is evident in a YouTube video that is ostensibly devoted to his childhood interest in maps, produced by the *New Yorker* in 2011.[37] The video opens with Shteyngart introducing himself as a "book writer" and describing his anxiety as a child in the United States and desire to return, if only imaginatively, to Leningrad: "I was a very—I guess obsessive-compulsive disorder I guess is the relevant disorder," he tells the camera, before comically regressing to a boyhood state as he plays with a toy airplane.[38] A key source of the video's appeal seems to be the privileges documented here, as the author indulges in favorite memories and casual reflections during seemingly abundant leisure time, and is understood as being important enough to command an audience while doing so. In other words this performance feeds curiosity about the kinds of rewards available to celebrities, while dramatizing the personality features ostensibly connected with literary success.

In this respect an intriguing tension seems to develop in Shteyngart's authorial persona—an inversion of Whitman's insistent claim to a success that he did not yet possess. In light of his obvious achievements, Shteyngart's continuing assumption of the role of "little failure" risks seeming incongruous rather than engagingly laughable. As Randy Boyagoda said of Shteyngart's memoir and the persona that has emerged in the work's book trailer: "it is here that *Little Failure* poses the first of its two challenges. For the book to work in its obsessive detailing of all that is congenitally hapless and pathetic about Shteyngart, we have to ignore the inconvenient fact of his impressive literary accomplishments and popularity, which too much depend upon the cultivation of this image: indeed, the very funny video trailer for *Little Failure* is all about Shteyngart's status as the literary world's greatest loser, but it happens to feature the hangdog author hamming it up alongside buddies James Franco and Jonathan Franzen."[39]

A recent article by Shteyngart published in the *New York Times Magazine* neatly illustrates his contemporary fusion of the elements of literary celebrity distinctive to Franklin, Whitman, and Twain's careers. Performing a piece of stunt journalism similar to that popularized by Hunter S. Thompson, Shteyngart spent a week watching nothing but Russian television, "piped in from three Apple laptops onto three 55-inch Samsung monitors in a room at the Four Seasons in Manhattan," the arrangement resembling "the trading floor of a very small hedge fund or the mission control of a poor nation's space program."[40] Like Misha Vainberg in *Absurdistan,* he was embosomed in luxury here—ordering expensive entrées and downing fine wines—as he absorbed a torrent of mass media, even calling in his psychotherapist for spiritual reinforcement.

Part of the appeal of this exercise is Shteyngart's status as a sort of Janus figure for a mainstream American audience—enough like them and of their sensibility to find Russian media weird and alarming, but different enough and steeped enough in ethnic bona fides to pass as a native informant, an authentic outside observer. The essay opened with Shteyngart's summary of the kitschy, homophobic content of a variety show, said to be illustrative of Russia's refusal to "succumb to the rest of the world's wimpy notions of tolerance."[41] The nation's television programming suggests its citizens' entrenched and baffling patriotism, centered as it is on the cult of Putin, and also their presumption of moral superiority to the permissive West. Just as Twain served as a spokesman for the wilder elements of the United States, chronicling his experiences of life on the frontier, Shteyngart has mediated here the wild East for Americans who may be curious about the region but only passingly familiar with its history and the peculiarities of its collective psychic life, or as much as the latter can be inferred from television anyway. He thus has offered crisp historical overviews of the Russian past and present, and acerbic analyses of its current leader and his apparently wide appeal. One is allowed to glimpse behind the unprecedentedly porous iron curtain and see the gaudy goings-on of contemporary Russian life denuded.

The terrible suffering of that life is made explicit in the article—Shteyngart noted, for instance, that one of his visitors' cousins had just been killed in Donetsk: "Nobody knows who killed him. There's no police. It's just anarchy."[42] But all such traumas are framed by the author's familiar half-ironic pose as depressive schlemiel, which gives everything learned about Russia an idiosyncratic character. In a kind of parodic, pessimistic mutation of Whitman's stance, Shteyngart's personality is offered as a portal to understanding others' experience. The complex dynamics of world history thus emerge out of the personal, which as always is pitched as both ludicrous and solemn. As Shteyngart wrote of his conversation with his psychotherapist, who visited him in his hotel, "In my books, I've tried to understand my parents and what they went through in the Soviet Union. . . . Maybe this project is another way to get to know them. Times change, regimes change, but the television stays pretty much the same."[43]

In this personalization of the Russian world, Shteyngart also seems to have told a Franklinian story of self-making—his own escape from "Putin's world" in the United States, where at last he could comfortably mediate his relationship with the past. Though nominally about his childhood home, Shteyngart's article also rather unsubtly affirms its own American patriotism, since Russian brutalities and *poshlost* are implicitly contrasted with the order and sanity of his adopted homeland. Finally, this is not the story of a first-generation immigrant, but a more generalized affirmation of American possibility and superiority. The great, truly preposterous villainy is located outside in what is finally a tyranny of the imagination: "Putin stands there, the centerpiece of his tableau, a contented man. Therein lies the brilliance of Russian television and why watching a week of it has been so painful. Unless you're a true believer, its endless din just reminds you of how alone you are in another man's designs. That man is Vladimir Vladimirovich Putin. These are his channels, his shows, his dreams and his faith."[44] Shteyngart becomes an inversion of the abused, silent guest he watched on a Russian talk show: "unlike a similar apparition on Jerry Springer, she never fights back even as the hosts and audience humiliate her. She sits there stoically, like a fallen character out of Dostoyevsky. In her own way, she is a model citizen for Putin's new Russia. She knows to keep her trap shut while being continuously shouted at by persons in authority."[45] Beyond its ironic gesturing, the article itself seems to confirm exactly this: the author's representative status as a liberated American who learned how to speak to authority in the American way. Transcending the ambivalence of Vladimir Girshkin in *The Russian Debutante's Handbook,* who could not stop dreaming of Eastern lands, Shteyngart can now simply mourn what happened there without him. Secure in a king-sized bed at the Four Seasons, with his psychoanalyst on call, he summoned forth reminders of what failure would have looked like, before resolutely sending them away: "Three satisfying clicks of three Samsung remotes and my whole week fades to black."[46]

Shteyngart has joked in recent interviews that, given the life expectancy of "Russian men," he may not have many good years left. But at just forty-four years old in 2016 and with a growing readership, he seems to be poised for a long and productive career. A television adaptation of *Super Sad True Love Story,* to be directed by Ben Stiller, is now in production, and the cinematic appeal of his satiric mode seems obvious. Shteyngart's next novel, titled *Hotel Solitaire,* is due out in 2017, and it will, if his description of it proves accurate, continue to break new ground: "At its heart 'Hotel Solitaire' is a family drama set in the high-stakes world of global finance, moving from upstate New York to Shanghai, Mumbai, Dubai. . . . It's about how power is disseminated in the world today and what happens when a spreadsheet jockey trades in her Excel for a Glock 22."[47] Such a narrative would mark a transition from the overtly autobiographical bent of the earlier writing, with *Little Failure* having filled in a remaining gap in the treatment of his early childhood in Leningrad, and would also move the setting of his writing further afield—beyond the United States and the post-Soviet states to regions that he has begun to explore already as a travel writer. The distribution of power in the contemporary world and the agency individuals might claim in abandoning one identity and assuming another have always been Shteyngart's essential themes.

NOTES

Chapter 1: Understanding Gary Shteyngart

1. Michiko Kakutani, "Welcome to America."
2. Shteyngart wrote in *Little Failure* (317):

> *The Russian Debutante's Handbook* . . . is if anything an unfaithful record of twenty-seven years of my life. It is filled with Nat Sherman cigarettes, guayabera shirts and janitor pants, words like 'venal' and 'aquiline,' cats named Kropotkin, dying beloved grandmothers, Eastern European castles brooding over urban hilltops, midwestern collegiate panic attacks, sedulous Jewish roommates from Pittsburgh, large female American backsides, cheerless Soviet cartoon crocodiles, eyebrow waxing, aged balsamic vinegar, and the age-old questions of whether it is better to be an alpha or a beta immigrant, and whether it's okay to bring others into the world when you are not happy with who you are. It is a catalog of the styles and snores of a particular era as recorded by an outsider fast becoming an insider. It is a very long document in which a troubled young man talks to himself. It is a collection of increasingly desperate jokes. To this day, some people tell me it's my best work, implying that it's all been kind of a downhill slog from there.

3. Ibid., 21.
4. Ibid., 51.
5. Olga Gershenson and David Schneer, "Soviet Jewishness and Cultural Studies," 139.
6. Ibid., 104.
7. Ibid., 117.
8. Gary Shteyngart, *Little Failure,* 145.
9. Ibid., 146.
10. Ibid., 159.
11. Ibid., 150.
12. Ibid., 217.
13. Ibid., 162.
14. Ibid., 162.
15. Ibid., 4.
16. Ibid., 253.
17. As Adrian Wanner has explained, "When Shteyngart sent Lee a chapter of *The Russian Debutante's Handbook* as part of an application to the creative writing

program at Hunter College, Lee was so impressed that he recommended the manuscript to his agent, who placed it with Riverhead Books, an imprint founded in 1995 with the specific multicultural purpose of incorporating 'potentially subaltern aesthetic and spiritual productions into the dominant national economy of entertainment commodities'" (*Out of Russia,* 130).

18. Gary Shteyngart, *Little Failure,* 32.

19. Ibid., 32.

20. Daniel Zalewski, "From Russia with Tsoris."

21. Nataša Kovačević, 154.

22. From 1948 to 1990, Prague was the capital of Czechoslovakia, a member of the Warsaw Pact, and thus under the influence of the Soviet Union. In 1993—the year during which Vladimir Girshkin, in the *Russian Debutante's Handbook,* visits Prava—the country was split in two, with Prague becoming the capital of the new Czech Republic.

23. Gary Shteyngart, *Absurdistan,* 113.

24. Gary Shteyngart, *Little Failure,* 55.

25. Anthony Giddens, *Runaway World,* 14.

26. Robert I. Friedman, *Red Mafiya.*

27. Gary Shteyngart, *The Russian Debutante's Handbook,* 188.

28. Gary Shteyngart, *Absurdistan,* 58.

29. Fainberg rose to broad public prominence after being profiled in the *Economist* in 1997 and has often been the subject of television documentaries investigating post-Soviet Mafiosi. See "Redfellas," *Economist* (March 15, 1997); Victor Malarek's *The Natashas: Inside the New Global Sex Trade* (Arcade Publishing, 2004); and the History Channel's 2006 documentary "The Russian Mafia."

30. Daniel Zalewski, "From Russia with Tsoris." By 2014 Shteyngart no longer claimed, as he had in the Zalewski article, to think of himself as "first and foremost a Russian"; in a 2014 interview with Renee Ghert-Zand, he gave the following answer when asked if he felt "like an American" now: "I feel like a New Yorker" (Ghert-Zand).

31. Alexandra Tatarsky, "Land of Plenty?"

32. Michael Hafford, "Little Failures."

33. Quoted in Edyta M. Bojanowska, *Nikolai Gogol,* 2.

34. Adrian Wanner, *Out of Russia,* 6–7.

35. Ibid., 139.

36. Ibid., 140.

37. Ibid., 142.

38. As Adam Rovner has noted, to another prominent "ethnic American author," Shteyngart's recognizable Jewishness was a particularly compelling aspect of his writing and a reason for helping to advance his career:

> Being in the majority in contemporary American literature means asserting one's minority affiliation and fragmented identity. . . . It is no surprise, therefore, that Chang-Rae [*sic*] Lee, the Korean American author whose debut novel, *Native Speaker,* is now a canonical work of Asian American literature, discovered Shteyngart. Or rather, Shteyngart discovered himself to Lee by mailing him his manuscript in an act of immigrant chutzpah that would make Abraham Cahan's David Levinsky proud. What attracted Lee to his protégé is equally telling. Lee marveled that "It's as if Woody Allen had been an immigrant. Compared to Shteyngart's novel, which vibrates with life, so much immigrant lit seems *so darned serious.*" And what could be more readily

> identifiable as Jewish in American culture than the figure of the schlemiel, embodied by Manhattan's most famous neurotic?"

In Rovner, "So Easily Assimilated," 322–23.

39. Quoted in Val Vinokur, "The Russians Came!"

40. Adrian Wanner, *Out of Russia,* 129.

41. Donald Weber, "Permutations of New-World Experiences Rejuvenate Jewish-American Literature."

42. See Marat Grinberg, "The Hollowing of Gary Shteyngart."

43. Adam Rovner, "So Easily Assimilated," 313. Rovner's title puns on a phrase, "immigrant chic," that was deployed by Irving Howe in 1986 to identify a nostalgia among American Jews for the cultural distinctiveness of older generations of Jewish immigrants. Howe is also famous for articulating in 1979 the so-called Howe Doctrine, which implied that Jewish American writing seemed to be on the decline given the successful assimilation, and hence the loss of distinctiveness, of contemporary Jews. For another incisive take on the legacy of the Howe Doctrine, see Michael P. Kramer's "Acts of Assimilation: The Invention of Jewish American Literary History." Shteyngart himself insisted on the assimilated status of American Jews today, in contrast to the situation of those from earlier generations. In his preface to Saul Bellow's novel *Ravelstein,* he wrote,

> As a Jew you are also an American, but somehow also not," Chick muses. I could well hear these words emerge from my father's mouth, and from others of his generation, and for [*sic*] a few bunkered-in Jewish stalwarts of my own. But how I disagree, generationally and experientially, with that line of thinking. In post-Seinfeldian, post–Larry-Davidian America, the very opposite could be inferred: "As an American you are also a Jew, but somehow also not." The fantasies of being pogrommed out of New Hampshire by an anti-Semitic militia nonetheless serve as a useful reminder of what post-Holocaust life was like for a generation of Jews who believed the ashes of the crematoria could one day fall upon the Berkshires."

Gary Shteyngart, "Bellow after Death."

44. Joe Moran, *Star Authors,* 102.

45. Michael Hafford, "Little Failures."

46. Gary Shteyngart, *Super Sad True Love Story,* 168.

Chapter 2: *The Russian Debutante's Handbook*

1. Gary Shteyngart, *The Russian Debutante's Handbook,* 16.

2. The "debutante" (with the feminine ending "e") of the title is apparently not meant to refer to Girshkin, or at least directly, but to his fellow Americans in Prava. As Adrian Wanner explained, "The world of the Russian aristocracy seemingly alluded to in the novel's title only surfaces in an ironic aside of the narrator, who compares a party among spoiled American expatriates in Eastern Europe to a nineteenth-century ball in the Russian provinces. But in a larger sense, Shteyngart was indeed 'coming out' with this book as a Russian debutant on the American literary stage, and . . . his novel has become a handbook for a whole new generation of post-Soviet immigrants with literary ambitions" (in Adrian Wanner, *Out of Russia*, 96).

3. Shteyngart, *The Russian Debutante's Handbook,* 3.

4. Ibid., 5.

5. *Prava*, with the accent on the last syllable, is also an alternate plural for *pravo*, "rights."

6. Kirkus Review, *The Russian Debutante's Handbook*.

7. Mendelsohn, "The Cool War."

8. Scott, "In the Shadow of Stalin's Foot."

9. Ibid.

10. Bahktin and Sollner, "Rabelais and Gogol," 48.

11. Antrim, "Coming-of-Age."

12. Borenstein, "Was It Sexy, or Just Soviet?" 33.

13. Friedman would more properly have said *North* American, since Bezmozgis is Canadian.

14. Friedman, "Nostalgia, Nationhood, and the New Immigrant Narrative," 77.

15. Ibid.

16. Rovner, "So Easily Assimilated," 318.

17. Kovačević, *Narrating Post/Communism*, 122.

18. Wanner, *Out of Russia*, 120.

19. Ibid., 121.

20. Shteyngart, *The Russian Debutante's Handbook*, 67.

21. This sense of fatedness in Vladimir, of being inexorably driven and agitated as a perpetual exile, was noted by Adam Rovner, who connected it to a pattern among recent Russian Jewish American writers (he invoked the familiar trio of Shteyngart, David Bezmozgis, and Lara Vapnyar) of emphasizing the distinctiveness of Jewish identity:

> There is much more to these books than a beggarly revelation of scars for the gratification of others. But significantly, these works expose the Jewish desire for acculturation while presenting an unmediated version of Jewish difference. The new immigrant chic suggests, perhaps wishfully, that Jews are not so easily assimilated—that they are essentially vulnerable, scared, or in some way physically marked as Other. . . . Shteyngart's Vladimir Girshkin is constantly identified as Jewish because of his physical features. His own mother, a grotesque amalgamation of crass parvenu types, says that he walks "like an old Jew from the shtetl," his "little Jew-walk" fit only for "Amatevka" or the "Vilnius ghetto." Later, Vladimir comes to identify his being a Russian Jew as synonymous with being a victim. His actions paint him as a schlemiel among the Russian mafiosos; his fate is to be beaten by skinheads at the behest of his boss, who is nonetheless "positively awed" by "persons of the Hebrew race" (in Adam Rovner, "So Easily Assimilated," 318).

22. Shteyngart, *The Russian Debutante's Handbook*, 77

23. Philip Roth, *Portnoy's Complaint*, 235. For a trenchant discussion of the role of the shiksa in Roth's work (and clues to how Shteyngart revised that role in his own novels), see Debra Shostak's "Roth and Gender" in *The Cambridge Companion to Philip Roth*. As Shostak wrote,

> Portnoy discovers that he does not possess his "wang" in his mature sexual encounters . . . because he remains under the cloud of the Jew/goy opposition. He seeks to transgress against the regulation of his Jewish body by sexual pursuit of a series of gentile women whom he hopes will afford him symbolic entry into American manhood. . . . The *shiksa*, the derogatory Yiddish term for the gentile woman, is for the Jewish man the highly eroticized image of cultural difference. A forbidden fruit,

the *shiksa* becomes an object of consumption analogous to the unkosher foods that tempt the Jew to disobey the rules that identify his body as Jewish and hence neither a "man" nor fully "American" (Shostak, "Roth and Gender," 116–17).

24. Shteyngart, *The Russian Debutante's Handbook,* 93.
25. Ibid., 103.
26. Ibid., 111.
27. Friedman, ""Nostalgia, Nationhood, and the New Immigrant Narrative" 77.
28. Ibid., 85.
29. Ibid., 42.
30. Ibid., 128.
31. Ibid., 132.
32. Ibid., 21.
33. Ibid., 45.
34. Ibid., 179.
35. Among his liberal friends in the American mainstream, Vladimir is taken to be a kind of symbol of multiculturalism and an assumed expert on all things Russian: "The inquisitive wanted to know: What was his prognosis for Russia following the Soviet Union's collapse? ('Not good.') Was he bitter about the new unipolar world? ('Yes, very.') Who was his favorite Communist? ('Bukharin, by a kilometer.') Was there any way to stop creeping capitalism and globalization? ('Not in my experience.')" From Gary Shteyngart, *The Russian Debutante's Handbook,* 73.
36. Ibid., 246
37. Nabokov, *Nicolai Gogol,* 70.
38. Ibid., 73.
39. I am grateful to Gennady Obatnin for pointing out Bulgakov's use of *poshlost* here. See "Two Hundred Years of *Poshlost*'" in *Understanding Russianness,* 190.
40. Bulgakov, *Unfading Light,* 187.
41. Gogol, *Dead Souls,* 251.
42. Phelps, *Essays on Russian Novelists,* 27.
43. Moynahan, *Vladimir Nabokov,* 36.
44. Lindberg, *Confidence Man,* 3.
45. Ibid., 7.
46. Shteyngart, *The Russian Debutante's Handbook,* 67. I am grateful to Anton Titov for suggesting a possible influence on Shteyngart here in the 1993 Russian film known in English as *A Window to Paris.* The plot involves the discovery of a portal allowing characters to travel directly from St. Petersburg to Paris, and the film investigates, among other themes taken up in *The Russian Debutante's Handbook,* the demoralized conditions of post-Soviet life, the repellent excesses of late capitalism, and the nostalgia of Russian expatriates for an idealized Soviet Union.
47. Ibid., 273.
48. Ibid., 214.
49. Ibid., 200.
50. Morgan's name, as so often is the case with Shteyngart's characters, seems to have a layered significance. She may be associated with Justin Morgan, who produced one of the first, and most iconic, of all American horse breeds, thus underscoring her status as a wholesome representative of the nation, and perhaps especially of its midwestern charms. However, as the woman who lures Vladimir away from his grand ambitions as

a "global leader" and into the dull refuge of Cleveland, she might also bring to mind a sort of ironic Morgan le Fay, the enchantress of Arthurian legend.

51. This fantastically large edifice evokes the Atlas statues outside the Hermitage Museum in St. Petersburg; the feet of these statues have often been photographed from angles that make it seem as though they are hundreds of times larger than the human figures who walk beyond them. In an essay tracking the uses made of Eastern European locales in recent American fiction, Jakob Ladegaard astutely noted the relevance of Gothic and Western motifs in Shteyngart's novel:

> [It] is the Western narrative that wins out in Gary Shteyngart's *The Russian Debutante's Handbook*. The codes of the Gothic are represented in this novel by a "giant and brooding" stone foot, a relic of a monstrous statue of Stalin that casts a shadow over the medieval centre of Prava (Shteyngart 2004, 193–94), recalling the Gothic tales about the Golem of Prague. The codes of the Western are embodied in Morgan, a strong, outdoor-loving Midwestern girl whom the comic Russian-American antihero, Vladimir, eventually marries. Morgan helps two melancholic young Stolovayans blow up the stone foot, for as one says: "before we can make this future we must take care of the sad history" (p. 382). Seeing it happen, Vladimir observes that the burning foot "was oddly reminiscent of the torch held aloft by the Statue of Liberty" (pp. 433–434). This apparently unironic comparison implies that Morgan acting as a true Western hero on behalf of the ideals of liberty and progress can finally free the locals from their authoritarian past. However, this "solution" seems a bit naïve when one recalls that all this—the tumbling of statues, the tearing down of walls—already happened once, while much remains ahead of the far more complex task of coming to terms with the way the past lives on in post-communist memories that cannot be erased with dynamite.

In "Cowboys and Vampires: Eastern European Encounters in New American Fiction," 47–48.

52. Shteyngart, *The Russian Debutante's Handbook,* 406.

53. A film version of the novel, starring Marlon Brando, was released in 1963.

54. Shteyngart, *The Russian Debutante's Handbook,* 307.

55. Lederer and Burdick, *Ugly American,* 123.

56. Ibid., 284.

57. Ibid., 385.

58. Boym, *Common Places,* 47.

59. Shteyngart, *The Russian Debutante's Handbook,* 374.

60. Boym, *Common Places,* 41.

61. Shteyngart, *The Russian Debutante's Handbook,* 390.

62. Ibid., 393.

63. The novel's distance from anything like strict realism is emphasized by its reliance on caricatures, its vagueness in describing everyday life in Prava, and even in such an odd and somewhat-distracting error as Vladimir's mention of a pile of discarded "bones" from emptied plates once holding the boneless dish chicken Kiev (196).

64. Shteyngart, *The Russian Debutante's Handbook,* 198.

65. Ibid., 404.

66. Intriguingly, *The Great Gatsby* itself has been identified recently as a novel of racial/ethnic "passing," with Gatsby understood as hiding his Jewish or African American

origins. See, for instance, Meredith Goldsmith, "White Skin, White Mask: Passing, Posing, and Performing in *The Great Gatsby*," 443–68.

67. Fitzgerald, *The Great Gatsby*, 192.

68. Shteyngart, *The Russian Debutante's Handbook*, 404.

69. Kovačević, *Narrating Post/Communism*, 148.

70. Gershenson and Schneer, "Soviet Jewishness," 130.

71. Shteyngart, *The Russian Debutante's Handbook*, 365.

72. Ibid., 366.

73. Ibid., 219.

74. Ibid., 185.

75. Ibid., 427.

76. Adam Rovner, "So Easily Assimilated," 324.

77. Morris Dickstein, "Questions of Identity," *The Writer Uprooted*, 125.

78. Jesper Reddig, "The Unbearable Whiteness of Being," *Mobile Narratives*, 222.

79. Gary Shteyngart, *The Russian Debutante's Handbook*, 475.

80. Ibid., 473. In *Little Failure*, Shteyngart recalls his youthful attempt to rewrite the Torah, and he cites this biblical passage as he puns on Cleveland as "Cleave-land": "God creates Adam (or, rather, Madman) and gives him a garden, called Cleaveland, referring, I'm guessing, both to the unsuccessful city in Ohio and Genesis 2:24 ('Therefore shall a man leave his father and his mother, and shall cleave unto his wife.')" From *Little Failure*, 159.

81. Ibid., 474.

82. Shteyngart, *The Russian Debutante's Handbook*, 472.

83. Ibid., 475.

84. Tennyson, "Ulysses," lines 1–7.

85. Ibid., line 11.

86. Shteyngart, *The Russian Debutante's Handbook*, 476.

Chapter 3: *Absurdistan*

1. With its abundant oil resources, widespread political corruption, and geographical positioning between Russia, Eastern Europe, and the Caspian Sea, Absurdsvanï seems modeled on Azerbaijan, a nation Shteyngart visited while researching this novel. A major difference, however, is that the majority of Azerbaijanis are Muslim.

2. Adrian Wanner, *Out of Russia*, 121.

3. Walter Kirn, "Russian Unorthodox."

4. Laura Miller, "Absurdistan."

5. Patrick Ness, "Absurd Person Singular."

6. Aleksandar Hemon, quoted in Gary Shteyngart's *Absurdistan*, back cover.

7. Steven S. Lee, "*Borat*, Multiculturalism, *Mnogonatsional'nost*," 32.

8. Dean J. Franco, "Globalization's Complaint," 171.

9. Olga Gershenson and David Schneer, "Soviet Jewishness and Cultural Studies," 142–43.

10. Adrian Wanner, *Out of Russia*, 131.

11. Peter Pomerantsev, *Nothing Is True*, 3.

12. Boris Vainberg's name seems to be a pun, moreover, on that of the infamous Ukrainian gangster Ludwig Fainberg, known for conspiring to purchase a Russian submarine in order to smuggle drugs into the United States, among other illicit activities.

13. Gary Shteyngart, *Absurdistan,* 57.
14. Ibid., 58.
15. Ibid., 56.
16. Ibid., 3.
17. Vladimir Nabokov, *Nicolai Gogol,* 67.
18. López, "Everybody else," 515.
19. Ibid., 510.
20. Gary Shteyngart, *Absurdistan*, vii.
21. Ibid., 6.
22. Ibid., 177.
23. Ibid., 289.
24. Ibid., 15.
25. Ibid., 46.
26. Ibid., 39.
27. Ibid., 152.
28. As Shteyngart remarked in an interview shortly after the publication of *Absurdistan*, "Shteynfarb is ostensibly me, but I hope is not. . . . When I teach, I try not to sleep with my funky students. Girshkin was a very autobiographical figure; he's not really in this book. He's just a side-gag." Quoted in Josh Lambert, "The True Name of Gary."
29. Adrian Wanner, *Out of Russia,* 129. Wanner noted that it might seem odd for someone who moved to the United States at the age of seven to think of himself as fundamentally Russian, as Shteyngart claims to, and that the author's often-caustic comments about his homeland might imply a sense of cultural alienation. However, as Wanner astutely pointed out, contempt for the conditions of everyday Russian life hardly excludes one from identifying as a Russian, since such contempt is common in canonical Russian literature, which Shteyngart clearly esteems highly, and consonant with a strategy among secular Russian Jews of affiliating themselves with Russian high culture in order to overcome discrimination.
30. Gary Shteyngart, *Absurdistan,* 54.
31. Ibid., 81.
32. Ibid., 176.
33. Wanner speculated that this character is in fact a parody of the "broken pseudo-Slavic English discourse used by [Jonathan Safran Foer's] Ukrainian narrator" in his novel *Everything Is Illuminated*. Adrian Wanner, *Out of Russia,* 9.
34. More subtle intertextual play exists in the novel's invocations of Nabokov. Misha's friend Alyosha-Bob insults Shteynfarb by claiming that "he thinks he's the Jewish Nabokov" (63). Several pages earlier, Misha noted how, as a child, he "briefly foresaw [his] parents' deaths—cancer ward, a ball of flame—and buried the knowledge deep in [his] then-tiny gut" (52), strongly echoing a famous passage from Nabokov's *Lolita:* "My very photogenic mother died in a freak accident (picnic, lightning) when I was three." *Lolita,* 10.
35. Ivan Turgenev, *Fathers and Sons,* 23.
36. Gary Shteyngart, *Absurdistan,* 17.
37. Zygmunt Bauman, *Identity,* 96.
38. Misha invokes here two or perhaps three Russian cultural icons: Kazimir Malevich (1878–1935), a painter and art theorist, and Arseny Tarkovsky (1907–1989), a poet and the father of Andrei Tarkovsky (1932–1986), a film director.
39. Gary Shteyngart, *Absurdistan,* 28.

40. Ibid., vii.

41. Ibid., 10.

42. Ibid., 32. As Simon Rogers suggested in a personal communication, Rouenna's homeland of Puerto Rico being a protectorate of the United States also seems to engage the notion of a parallel between Russian and American imperialism.

43. Ibid., 35.

44. Philip Roth, *Portnoy's Complaint,* 235.

45. Gary Shteyngart, *Absurdistan,* 79.

46. The German-language edition of *Absurdistan* was published as *Snack Daddys abenteuerliche Reise* ("Snack Daddy's Adventurous Journey"), thus emphasizing the importance of Misha's alias to the novel and of hip-hop culture more generally.

47. Gary Shteyngart, *Absurdistan,* 6.

48. Ibid., 90.

49. Ibid. 5. Misha's apparent cluelessness about American racial experience is suggested when he remarks on the ostensible similarity between Goncharov's idle landowner—who has the luxury of "giving up on life" because of his inherited fortune—and African Americans living in what was then a seedy section of New York: "The Oblomov inside me has always been fascinated by people who are just about ready to give up on life, and in 1990, Brooklyn was an Oblomovian paradise." *Absurdistan,* 19. A possible influence on Shteyngart in his construction of Misha is—as Anton Titov suggested in a private communication—the Jewish Russian hip-hop artist known as Timoti (Timur Ildarovich Yunusov). In order to emphasize his own outsider status among the ultra-rich citizens of "New Russia," Timoti often cites his Tatar roots, and he has sought high-profile affiliations with American artists such as Snoop Dogg.

50. Ibid., 88.

51. Ibid., 56.

52. Ibid., 126.

53. Ibid., 158.

54. Ibid., 37.

55. Ibid., 60.

56. Steven S. Lee, "*Borat,* Multiculturalism, *Mnogonatsional'nost,*" 22, 31.

57. Ibid., 251.

58. Ibid., 251.

59. Horowitz, "I'm a Uniter, Not a Divider."

60. Gary Shteyngart, *Absurdistan,* 255.

61. Shteyngart sets his book just before September 11, 2001, and clearly has in mind the American intervention in Iraq and the allegations of cynical warmongering leveled against American multinational corporations such as Halliburton. As Alexandra Tatarsky pointed out, "Gary Shteyngart's first novel, often considered the book which heralded Russian immigrant fiction, was published just one year after the fall of the twin towers, the physical and symbolic collapse of America's economic centre. Its aftermath had meant the re-examination of the American dream in an era of increased income disparity, unemployment, and student debt, in cities rapidly rendered unrecognisable by gentrification and corporatization." In Alexandra Tatarsky, "Land of Plenty?" These scenes in *Absurdistan* also seem to echo, in their descriptions of a city being shelled "for its own good," not just Heller's work but an infamous statement reported by the Associated Press during the Vietnam War. According to the correspondent Peter Arnett, a "United States major" claimed that "it became necessary to destroy the town [Bến

Tre] to save it": The major "was talking about the decision by allied commanders to bomb and shell the town regardless of civilian casualties, to rout the Vietcong." In Peter Arnett's "Major Describes Move."

62. Gary Shteyngart, *Absurdistan*, 255.
63. Ibid., 309.
64. Ibid., 269.
65. Ibid., 236.
66. Ibid., 191.
67. Antone Minard, *Jesus in History, Legend, and Scripture*, 497–98
68. Ibid., 498.
69. Ibid., 498.
70. Mark Twain, *The Adventures of Huckleberry Finn*, 121–22.
71. Gary Shteyngart, *Absurdistan*, 193.
72. Ibid., 191.
73. Dostoevsky, *The Brothers Karamazov*, 385.
74. Weinberg, "A Designer Universe?"
75. Gary Shteyngart, *Absurdistan*, viii. Shteyngart has described his own relationship to Judaism in similar terms, as in this interview, "The True Name of Gary," with Josh Lambert:

> [Lambert:] The impression I get from what I've read of your work, and other interviews, is that you're not a fan of Jewish institutions—day schools, synagogues, etcetera.
>
> [Shteyngart:] Well . . . I read Hebrew. I've gone through the whole [Jewish day school] thing. I prayed my little head out. I believed so much in this. It was interesting: I was treated like shit, and yet I still believed. It was a typical Russian mentality: you know, the more they whip you, the more you—I remember scouring the house for *chometz*.
> It's not just Judaism. It's religion in general. In my books, I wail on Judaism and Christianity. Islam takes care of itself—I don't need to do anything with Islam.
>
> [Lambert:] At the same time, you've received at least two Jewish book prizes—and I assume you wouldn't say no to more.
>
> [Shteyngart:] I don't say no to any of this. No, no—look. I'm a Jewish writer, there's no doubt. I just don't believe in no Yahweh.

76. Ibid., 251.
77. Ibid., 17.
78. Ibid., 23.
79. Here Shteyngart seems to draw on a traumatic personal experience, his own circumcision at the age of eight: "The Stinky Russian Bear, the second most hated boy in first and soon to be second grade of Hebrew school . . . is lying, his crotch exposed, in his parents' bed with what feels like razor blades cutting through his penis, over and over again. (It goes without saying that the procedure at the public hospital did not go well.) There will be creatures in horror movies in my near future, the softshell crabs of Ridley Scott's *Alien* the most visually accomplished ones, but this baroque chiaroscuro of dried blood and thread will never find equal. And, to this day, whenever I see a naked blade, I shudder because I know what it can do to a boy of eight." From Gary Shteyngart's *Little Failure*, 117.

80. Ibid., 106–7.

81. Adrian Wanner, *Out of Russia,* 128.

82. Olga Gershenson and David Schneer, 142.

83. Gary Shteyngart, *Absurdistan,* 114. In a discussion touching on the representation of Jews in *The Russian Debutante's Handbook,* Adam Rovner noted with some concern Shteyngart's and other Jewish authors' insistence that Jews are marked out by physical alterity: "Jews are different, these works suggest, because of blood and birth, because of gender or sexual orientation, or because of appearance and temperament. It is particularly surprising that younger American Jewish writers would betray an obsession with a supposed Jewish physical essence, given that this echoes a trope of antisemitism. Perhaps they may even be expressing a nostalgia for *enforced* difference." In "The *New* Immigrant Chic," 321.

84. Walter Kirn, in his overwhelmingly positive *New York Times* review, also expressed some uneasiness with Shteyngart's caricatures of ethnic identity—as well as a good deal of admiration for it:

> There are a lot of stereotypes here and plenty of intellectually incorrect exercises in racial and group determinism. Shteyngart, via Misha, thinks in peoples, not just individuals. He jokes in peoples, too, and not only about Jews and Russians, as his heritage entitles him to, but about Muslims, Germans, Brooklynites and every other in-group he can outrage. One envies his sense of entitlement to biases, and his frank understanding of the fact that such crude distinctions make the world go round. Especially these days, when they're not supposed to. When, ostensibly, we're all United Nations blue.

From Walter Kirn, "Russian Unorthodox."

85. Gary Shteyngart, *Absurdistan,* 91.

86. Ibid., 194.

87. Ibid., 187. Shteyngart mentions in a 2002 interview that he experienced a similar encounter while visiting *Azerbaijan:* "This is Baku. . . . Last year on the promenade here, I was sitting on a bench, taking a break from finishing my novel. A woman approached, offering herself for $5. When I said no, she offered to include her 5-year-old daughter." Quoted in Daniel Zalewski, "From Russia with Tsoris."

88. Gary Shteyngart, *Absurdistan,* 328.

89. Ibid., 332.

90. Dean J. Franco, "Globalization's Complaint," 179.

91. Gary Shteyngart, *Absurdistan,* 333.

92. Ibid., 333.

Chapter 4: *Super Sad True Love Story*

1. These videos can be found here: https://www.youtube.com/watch?v=EfzuOu4UIOU, and here: https://www.youtube.com/watch?v=DwWToVgnCCw (accessed July 20, 2015).

2. Gary Shteyngart, *Super Sad True Love Story,* 5.

3. In his memoir Shteyngart explains the significance of this name to his father and its uncanny appearance in his own work:

> [In my childhood,] my father has a best friend his age. A non-Jewish kid named Lionya. When he is three years old, my father's best friend dies of some unspecified

> war-related disease. This is my father's third [childhood] memory: Lionya's funeral. My father tells me of Lionya's existence during the spring of 2011. "Lionya," short for "Leonid," is a fairly unremarkable Russian name, but in my first novel, published in 2002, the childhood friend of the novel's hero, Vladimir Girshkin, happens to be Lionya, and indeed, he is one of the few truly sympathetic people in the book (together Vladimir and Lionya share a batch of Little Red Riding Hood candies given by Vladimir's mother and fall asleep side by side on a Soviet kindergarten mat). In my third novel, published in 2010, "Lionya" is the Russian name of one of the two main characters, Lenny Abramov. Without knowing who he was, I have spent half my life honoring Lionya in prose.

From Gary Shteyngart, *Little Failure,* 38.

4. Gary Shteyngart, *Super Sad True Love Story,* 3.

5. See http://www.blueletterbible.org/lang/lexicon/lexicon.cfm?strongs=H7311 (accessed July 20, 2015).

6. Gary Shteyngart, *Super Sad True Love Story,* 5. Shteyngart notes in his acknowledgments that his explorations of the "post-human" were influenced by the anti-aging and futurist gurus Ray Kurzweil and Aubrey de Grey, who have written extensively on the possibility of, and the means of achieving, eternal human life.

7. Lenny's father cites the etymology of Eunice's name during their meeting at a family dinner: "My parents sat down, and my father proposed a seasonal toast in English: 'To the Creator, who created America, the land of free, and who give us Rubenstein, who kill Arab, and to love which is blooming in such times between my son and Yooo-neee-kay, who [big wink to Eunice] will be victorious, like Sparta over Athens.'" 138–39. This invocation of the Greek city-states may also ironically suggest a coming defeat for the United States (an analogue of "free," democratic Athens) in its political and economic struggle with China (a stand-in for "communist" Sparta).

8. Marleen S. Barr, in an essay exploring Shteyngart's playfulness with utopian schemes gone awry, argued that the novel is

> a specifically New York Jewish dystopia that is tinged with utopian elements. . . . Lenny is a financially secure Everyman inhabitant of his world. In the context of Russian Jews facing pogroms and Nazis murdering European Jews, being a secure Everyman Jew is a utopian success story. Lenny's ordinariness is signalled by his choice to drive on the Long Island Expressway (Shteyngart 284) rather than the Queens transportation artery that really is called Utopia Parkway. Utopia Parkway borders a Queens neighbourhood, predominantly inhabited by Jews, called Utopia. The Jewish Queens neighbourhood called Utopia is a real utopian achievement. Lenny inhabits a New York City world that is a utopian haven for Jews.

In Barr, "America and Books Are 'Never Going to Die,'" 312–14. Barr posited Eunice, moreover, as another reworking of the *shiksa* figure made notorious in the fiction of Philip Roth: "As *Portnoy's Complaint* exemplifies, for Roth's generation Jewish male transgression manifested itself as romantic involvement with a blond *shiksa.* For Shteyngart's generation, dating and marrying Caucasian *shiksas* is normal, not transgressive. The present-day young Jewish male who does not want to marry a clone of his mother must now be involved in an interracial relationship, all the better if the woman practises a religion that is more exotic than Christianity. Korean Eunice Park fits the bill as the new Jewish male utopian fantasy meta-*shiksa*" (in Barr, "America and Books," 313).

9. Gary Shteyngart, *The Russian Debutante's Handbook,* 54.
10. Ibid., 95.
11. Zygmunt Bauman, *Identity,* 96.
12. Gary Shteyngart, *Super Sad True Love Story,* 136. Lenny's attitude to his Russian heritage for the most part is one of suppression. As he reveals while feeling vulnerable to imposing security agents on his flight home from Italy: "My parents were born in what used to be the Soviet Union, and my grandmother had survived the last years of Stalin, although barely, but I lack the genetic instinct to deal with unbridled authority. Before a greater force, I crumble. And so, as my hand began the long journey from my lap into the fear-saturated cabin air, I wanted my parents near me. I wanted my mother's hand on the back of my neck, the cool touch that always calmed me down as a child. I wanted to hear my parents' Russian spoken aloud, because I always thought of it as the language of cunning acquiescence" (ibid., 41.)
13. Ibid., 64.
14. Ibid., 120.
15. Lenny reminds us that his father suffered the "humiliation of growing up a Jew in the Soviet Union" (321), but in the contemporary United States, Jewish and American have, at least for some, come to seem synonymous, as in the following diatribe launched at Lenny by an embittered American expatriate: "He's not like us. He's a real American. A real sharpie. He's the reason why we're in Venezuela right now. He's why people are afraid to say 'boo' in the States. He's no better than Rubenstein. Look at those dark, lying Ashkenazi eyes. Kissinger the Second" (20). Shteyngart's no doubt partly ironic representation of American Jews as fully assimilated—and in fact representative of a hegemonic culture—would seem to mock the nostalgia for Jewish marginality identified by Adam Rovner and others as a prominent element of some contemporary Jewish American fiction, including Shteyngart's own *The Russian Debutante's Handbook*. See Rovner, "So Easily Assimilated."
16. Ibid., 51.
17. Ibid., 216.
18. Michael Wood, "Never Say Die."
19. Michiko Kakutani, "Love Found Amid Ruins of Empire."
20. Thier, "Love and Hardship."
21. Annie McClanahan, "Bad Credit," 34.
22. Ulla Kriebernegg, "Ending Aging," 62.
23. Anonymous, "Finance and Economics," 85.
24. Carolyn Marvin, ""Your Smart Phones Are Hot Pockets to Us," 156.
25. Laurence J. Kirmayer, Eugene Raikhel, and Sadeq Rahimi, "Cultures of the Internet," 170.
26. Gary Shteyngart, *Super Sad True Love Story,* 19. In *Little Failure,* Shteyngart tells of reading *1984* in the year 1984 and of being particularly influenced by the novel's scenes of torture: "I commit the passages in which O'Brien tortures Winston to memory. When the kid [a vulnerable neighbor he will bully] is alone staring sullenly at a comic book over a picnic table, I approach him. I sit down and begin to speak in measured tones. 'Power is not a means, Vinston; it is an end. One does not establish a dictatorship in order to safeguard a revolution; one makes the revolution in order to establish the dictatorship. The object of persecution is persecution. The object of torture is torture. The object of power is power'" (175–76).
27. Ibid., 7–9.

28. Ibid., 43. The capital letters in these announcements evoke the official signage Shteyngart recalls from his childhood in Soviet Leningrad. See *Little Failure*, 53.

29. Milan Kundera, *Unbearable Lightness of Being*, 133.

30. Ibid., 136.

31. Ibid., 229.

32. Gary Shteyngart, *Super Sad True Love Story*, 275.

33. Milan Kundera, *Unbearable Lightness of Being*, 249.

34. Ibid., 253.

35. Gary Shteyngart, *Super Sad True Love Story*, 44.

36. Walter Benjamin, "Moscow," 30.

37. Gary Shteyngart, *Super Sad True Love Story*, 57.

38. Ibid., 78.

39. As Annie McClanahan explains of the kind of subjectivity created by this comprehensive collection and publication of personal data:

> The novel's use of data-caricature elegantly registers contemporary credit scoring's treatment of individuals as bundles of information. The alienating experience of "not me" one experiences on encountering one's caricatured personification by credit data is not the anxiety of a reduction but the anxiety of an excess-the experience of being understood as "quantitative granularity," of being defined not by a carefully limited array of personal details but by an indefinite accumulation of data. Under such conditions, we are left with something like what Gilles Deleuze famously called "dividuals," the divided data bodies of late capitalism, atomized persons whose lack of coherence or consistency can only be registered by caricature's excess of detail and data (in "Bad Credit," 44).

40. Gary Shteyngart, *Super Sad True Love Story*, 277.

41. Ibid., 270.

42. Ray Kurweil, *The Age of Intelligent Machines*, 447.

43. Marvin, who used Shteyngart's novel to illustrate some of her arguments about the social consequences of the digital age, pointed to the problems of "asymmetric transparency"—that is, the ways in which users of networking technology are made visible as well as vulnerable to those with whom they connect, a circumstance that can be especially insidious when citizens are targeted by powerful organizations: "Asymmetric transparency also tilts the surveillance advantage toward stalker/trackers and away from targets unaware of their own visibility. . . . Even digital savviness offers scant protection from software algorithms and actuated devices meant to steer consumption and other choices. The state's insatiable appetite for information about citizens digitally cast as the already- or soon-to-be-suspected shreds expectations for privacy." From Carolyn Marvin's "Your Smart Phones," 156.

44. Alexis de Tocqueville, *Democracy in America*, 2.1.2.520.

45. Ibid., 520.

46. Gary Shteyngart, *Little Failure*, 93.

47. Gary Shteyngart, *Super Sad True Love Story*, 44. Another kind of totalitarianism can be felt in the way individuals are relentlessly expected to engage in, and risk the negative judgements that might come from, public "performances." While Shteyngart's satire aptly captures the toxicity of such social pressures as they apply to all citizens, it seems less well-targeted in relation to the striking vulnerability of young women in an ostensibly permissive youth culture. In a message to Eunice, for instance, a character

nicknamed "Grillbitch" reports that a rival of hers had ended up being recorded having group sex at a party and that after the video was made public by others, her "ratings went up" (29)—confirming, in other words, her social success. Such popularity may be a cliché of contemporary celebrity culture—and this seems to be Shteyngart's point—but its representation here ignores the brutal conditions of public shaming that routinely attend young women's exposure in similar circumstances, such as the tragic case of Rehtaeh Parsons. The gender inequalities in our hypersexualized, hypermediated culture do not seem fairly acknowledged in the novel's satiric vision.

48. Ibid., 86.

49. Ibid., 27.

50. Ibid., 186.

51. Ibid., 127.

52. Vladimir Nabokov, *Lolita,* 141.

53. Gary Shteyngart, *Super Sad True Love Story,* 25.

54. Ibid., 111.

55. Ibid., 22.

56. Ibid., 52.

57. Gary Shteyngart, *Little Failure,* 3.

58. Gary Shteyngart, *Super Sad True Love Story,* 62.

59. Ibid., 304.

60. Ibid., 187.

61. Ibid., 190.

62. Ibid.

63. Ibid., 65.

64. Ibid., 80.

65. Ibid., 6.

66. Ibid., 56.

67. Ibid., 60.

68. Gary Shteyngart, *Little Failure,* 157. Another pop-cultural influence from Shteyngart's youth seems at play here too; as he notes in his memoir of seeing the movie *Cocoon:* "The theme of the movie is immortality. 'We'll never be sick,' the Wilford Brimley character tells his grandson before the aliens beam him up. 'We won't get any older, and we'll never die.' . . . I want Wilford Brimley to be my grandpa, and I want him to die. I keep thinking about what he tells his slabyi obsessive little grandson at the start of the film: 'The trouble with you is you think too much and that's when a guy gets scared'" (from *Little Failure,* 168).

69. Michael Wood, "Never Say Die."

70. Gary Shteyngart, *Super Sad True Love Story,* 216–17. *Soylent Green* (1973) is set, like *Super Sad True Love Story,* in a near-future, dystopian New York. Amid overcrowding and starvation, a corporation sells a food source manufactured out of human remains. In *Logan's Run* (1976), a science-fiction film set in the twenty-third century, the "old"—that is, anyone over thirty—are killed off in order to ease overpopulation.

71. Gary Shteyngart, *Super Sad True Love Story,* 219.

72. Ibid., 63.

73. F. Scott Fitzgerald, *The Great Gatsby,* 49.

74. Gary Shteyngart, *Super Sad True Love Story,* 221.

75. F. Scott Fitzgerald, *The Great Gatsby,* 106.

76. Gary Shteyngart, *Super Sad True Love Story,* 269.

77. Shteyngart puns on that history further in Lenny's description of his corporation's nicknames for its different departments: "We have this Cowboys and Indian thing going on at Post-Human Services. At the Life Lovers Outreach division we call ourselves Cowboys; the 'Indians' are the actual research staff, mostly on loan from the Subcontinent and East Asia, housed at an eighty-thousand-square-foot facility on York and at three satellite locations in Austin, Texas; Concord, Massachusetts; and Portland, Oregon." 123–24. The three satellite locations cited here provide an illustrative triangulation of national ideals and geographical expansion, from the seat of Transcendentalism in Concord, to the nineteenth-century frontiers where major battles between "Cowboys and Indians" took place in the Southwest and Northwest.

78. Milan Kundera, *Unbearable Lightness of Being,* 176.

79. Gary Shteyngart, *Super Sad True Love Story,* 181.

80. Thomas Jefferson, "First Inaugural," 493.

81. Abraham Lincoln, *Abraham Lincoln: His Speeches and Writings,*41.

82. Gary Shteyngart, *Super Sad True Love Story,* 328.

83. Ibid., 331.

84. F. Scott Fitzgerald, *The Great Gatsby,* 171.

85. Ruth Franklin, "Dechronification."

86. Vladimir Nabokov, *Lolita,* 148.

87. Ibid., 29.

88. Ibid., 284.

89. Gary Shteyngart, *Super Sad True Love Story,* 53.

90. Ibid., 273.

91. Ibid., 297.

Chapter 5: *Little Failure*

1. The trailer for *Little Failure* can be found here: https://www.youtube.com/watch?v=sowt9Wq7zYU (accessed July 6, 2015).

2. Yevgeniya Traps, "The Year of the Former Soviet Author." Curiously, translations of Russian works have not enjoyed the same popularity as works by Russian Americans. As Owen Matthews has related: "Noble efforts to translate and promote Russia's contemporary literature persist, but today in the United States, only about 4.6 percent of books translated into English were written in Russian, placing the language far behind French, Spanish, and German. 'Great books are being written in Russia today,' Dmitry Bykov, Russia's leading contemporary critic and a biographer of Pasternak, said in a radio interview. 'But not nearly enough get translated'" (in "Pasternak's Shadow," 84).

3. The pun here is, of course, on the "Beat Generation," the group of American beatnik writers that included Jack Kerouac, Allen Ginsberg, and William Burroughs, with a nod to the beetroot, which is typically included in borscht, a traditional soup often served in Russian and Eastern European homes.

4. From Simon & Schuster Canada's site, "Russian Tattoo: A Memoir."

5. From Penguin Random House's site, "A Backpack, a Bear, and Eight Crates of Vodka."

6. Alexandra Tatarsky, "Land of Plenty?" Reflecting on the "unprecedented boom in recent years" of Russian American writing and how its authors have been evolving in their response to it, Adrian Wanner has noted that "a certain weariness has settled in among some of the providers of these Russian-American narratives. While these authors have benefitted from the appeal of ethnic and multicultural products on the U.S. literary

market, they also risk being trapped in an 'exotic' niche and becoming purveyors of predictable plots. . . . Two Soviet-born American authors, Keith Gessen and Michael Idov . . . have been bucking the trend by refusing to openly play the 'Russian card,' the 'Jewish card,' or the 'immigrant card' in their fictional work" (in "Moving beyond the Russian-American Ghetto: The Fiction of Keith Gessen and Michael Idov," 281–82).

7. From W. W. Norton & Company's site, "Midnight in Siberia."
8. From Public Affairs' site, "Nothing Is True and Everything Is Possible."
9. Andy Borowitz, "Mr. Shteyngart's Planet," 9.
10. Meg Wolitzer, "Gary Shteyngart's."
11. Jennie Yabroff, "The Weight of the Past."
12. Randy Boyagoda, "'Little Failure,' by Gary Shteyngart."
13. Gary Shteyngart, *Little Failure,* 317.
14. Ibid., 317.
15. Quoted in Michael Hafford, "Little Failures."
16. Gary Shteyngart, *Little Failure,* 130.
17. Ibid., 33.
18. Ibid., 34.
19. Ibid.
20. Ibid., 62.
21. Ibid., 95.
22. Ibid., 99.
23. Ibid., 137.
24. Ibid., 317.
25. Ibid.
26. Ibid., 318.
27. Ibid., 30–31.
28. Ibid., 41.
29. Ibid., 30.
30. Ibid., 340.
31. Ibid., 318–19.
32. Ibid., 320.
33. Ibid.
34. Sean Redmond, "The Star," 109–10.
35. Ibid., 316.
36. Ibid., 119.
37. Ibid., 109.
38. Ibid., 224.
39. Ibid., 226.
40. Ibid., 254.
41. Gary Shteyngart, *The Russian Debutante's Handbook,* 271.
42. Gary Shteyngart, *Little Failure,* 256.
43. Ibid., 279.
44. Ibid.
45. Gary Shteyngart, "The New Two-Way," 290.
46. Zygmunt Bauman, *Identity,* 19.
47. Daniel Zalewski, "From Russia with Tsoris."
48. Gary Shteyngart, *Little Failure,* 203.
49. Marat Grinberg, "The Hollowing of Gary Shteyngart," 69.

50. Ibid., 71.
51. Ibid.
52. Gary Shteyngart, *The Russian Debutante's Handbook*, 42.
53. Gary Shteyngart, *Absurdistan*, 329.
54. Gary Shteyngart, *Super Sad True Love Story*, 11.
55. Ibid., 135.
56. Gary Shteyngart, *Super Sad True Love Story*, 11–12.
57. Ibid., 136.
58. Gary Shteyngart, *Little Failure*, 107.
59. Ibid., 107.
60. Ibid., 117.
61. Quoted in Renee Ghert-Zand, "Shteyngart's memoir."
62. Yuri Slezkine, *The Jewish Century*, 127.
63. Gary Shteyngart, *Little Failure*, 279.
64. Ibid., 139.
65. Ibid., 140.
66. Ibid., 7–8.
67. Ibid., 342.
68. Ibid., 313.
69. As Barry King remarked of the religious legacy evident in contemporary confessional media: "Reality shows and talkshows, and the co-dependent sites and practices of celebrity gossip, draw on the confession heritage of the Church for a set of background expectancies of what constitutes a 'true' confession, in order to nurture popular interest and engagement. The confessional ideal lives on in the notion of authenticity and the unquestioned value of openness that is the raison d'être of 'therapeutic' television" (in "Stardom, Celebrity and the Para-Confession," 120).

Chapter 6: Gary Shteyngart and American Literary Celebrity

1. Kate Gwynne, "10 Authors Who Excel on the Internet."
2. Ibid.
3. Ibid.
4. Katy Waldman, "It's Time to Stop Praising Authors for 'Being Good at the Internet.'"
5. See the *Little Failure* trailer here: https://www.youtube.com/watch?v=sowt9Wq7zYU (accessed July 6, 2015).
6. Walter Isaacson, *Benjamin Franklin: An American Life*, 328.
7. See Penguin Random House, "Little Failure: A Memoir."
8. AF, "Girl at War," *Saturday Paper*, 30 May 2015. https://www.thesaturdaypaper.com.au/2015/05/31/girl-war/14329080001928 (accessed August 2, 2015).
9. Jacob Silverman runs a Tumblr blog devoted to these blurbs: http://shteyngartblurbs.tumblr.com/. Shteyngart's "open letter" can be found here: http://www.newyorker.com/books/page-turner/an-open-letter-from-gary-shteyngart (accessed July 28, 2015).
10. The documentary can be found here: https://www.youtube.com/watch?t=72&v=gze77JyKcoU (accessed July 28, 2015).
11. See http://shteyngartblurbs.tumblr.com/ (accessed July 28, 2015).
12. See http://shteyngartblurbs.tumblr.com/page/2 (accessed July 28, 2015).
13. Nabokov punningly changed the spelling of the word in his own deployment of it: "I find it preferable to transcribe that fat brute of a word thus: poshlust—which renders

in a somewhat more adequate manner the dull sound of the second, neutral 'o.' Inversely the first 'o' is as big as the plop of an elephant falling into a muddy pond and as round as the bosom of a bathing beauty on a German picture postcard." See *Nicolai Gogol* by Vladimir Nabokov (New York: New Directions, 1961), 63.

14. Vladimir Nabokov, Nicolai, 68.

15. Joe Moran in *Star Authors: Literary Celebrity in America*, 18.

16. See chapter 2 for a brief consideration of some of the similarities between *The Russian Debutante's Handbook* and Twain's *Adventures of Huckleberry Finn*.

17. Justin Kaplan, *Mr. Clemens and Mark Twain,* Preface.

18. Loren Glass, *Authors Inc.: Literary Celebrity in the Modern United States, 1880–1980*, 70.

19. Shteyngart, quoted in Renee Ghert-Zhand, "Shteyngart's Memoir 'Little Failure' Is Great Success."

20. Troy Patterson, "Three Days of Vodka with Gary Shteyngart."

21. Adrian Wanner, *Out of Russia*, 133.

22. Adrian Wanner, *Out of Russia,* 133.

23. Ibid., 130.

24. Gary Shteyngart, *Absurdistan,* 11.

25. Adam Rovner, "The New Immigrant Chic," 318.

26. Ibid., 322.

27. Gary Shteyngart, *Little Failure,* 87.

28. Gary Shteyngart, *Absurdistan,* 135–36.

29. Gary Shteyngart, *Super Sad True Love Story,* 296.

30. Gary Shteyngart, "O.K., Glass."

31. David Haven Blake, *Walt Whitman and the Culture of American Celebrity,* 3.

32. Ibid., 42.

33. Walt Whitman, "Song of Myself," lns 97–98.

34. Gary Shteyngart, *Little Failure,* 318.

35. There are obvious and intriguing similarities between Shteyngart's public persona and that of Woody Allen, especially Allen's in the 1970s. Both play the role of a neurotic New York schlemiel with a penchant for self-disclosure tied to experience with psychoanalysis. In his *New Yorker* profile from 2011, Shteyngart almost seems to be emulating the opening monologue from Allen's *Annie Hall.* Chang-rae Lee, the Korean American author who helped launch Shteyngart, was perhaps the first to make the Allen comparison, remarking of his student's career that "it's as if Woody Allen were an immigrant." "Immigrants Have to Be Nuts," *Scotsman,* 21 July 2007. http://www.scotsman.com/lifestyle/culture/books/immigrants-have-to-be-nuts-1–909950 (accessed July 25, 2015).

36. Gary Shteyngart, "The New Moscow."

37. *New Yorker*, "Gary Shteyngart Describes."

38. Shteyngart has described this boyhood fantasizing in *Little Failure*: "When I feel sad from Hebrew school, I turn to my Soviet atlas and an Eastern Air Lines toy plane my mother bought for half a dollar on Fourteenth Street, the boulevard of discount dreams in faraway Manhattan. . . . I launch my plane down the runway of our cluttered apartment, then I sit there with the plane in my hand for the eight and a half hours it takes to get to Rome, humming to myself the sounds of the jet engine" (106–7).

39. Randy Boyagoda, "'Little Failure,' by Gary Shteyngart."

40. Gary Shteyngart, "Out of My Mouth."

41. Ibid.

42. Ibid.

43. Ibid.

44. Ibid. One of the ironies here is that the televisual spectacles Shteyngart has described are themselves fervent imitations of American television. As Peter Pomerantsev pointed out, in the decades since the Soviet collapse, Russia paradoxically has striven to mimic Western media as a way to maintain a certain cultural autonomy—or at least political hegemony—via propaganda: "In a country covering nine time zones, one-sixth of the world's land mass, stretching from the Pacific to the Baltic, from the Arctic to the Central Asian deserts, from near-medieval villages where people still draw water from wooden wells by hand, through single-factory towns and back to the blue glass and steel skyscrapers of the new Moscow—TV is the only force that can unify and rule and bind this country. It's the central mechanism of a new type of authoritarianism, one far subtler than twentieth-century strains" (from Peter Pomerantsev, *Nothing Is True*, 5).

45. Ibid.

46. Ibid.

47. Quoted in Julie Bosman, "New Novel from Shteyngart Will Be an 'International Thriller.'"

BIBLIOGRAPHY

Works by Shteyngart

The Russian Debutante's Handbook. New York: Berkeley Publishing Group, 2002.

"Several Anecdotes about My Wife." *Granta* 78 (June 28, 2002). http://granta.com/several-anecdotes-about-my-wife/ (accessed April 20, 2016).

"Planet of the Yids." *Granta* 93 (April 3, 2006). http://granta.com/planet-of-the-yids/ (accessed April 20, 2016).

"From the Diaries of Lenny Abramov." *Granta* 97 (April 16, 2007). http://granta.com/from-the-diaries-of-lenny-abramov/ (accessed April 20, 2016).

"Portrait of My Father." *Granta* 104 (February 12, 2009). http://granta.com/issues/granta-104-fathers/ (accessed April 20, 2016).

"The Mother Tongue between Two Slices of Rye." *The Genius of Language*. Ed. Wendy Lesser. New York: Pantheon Books, 2004.

"The New Two-Way Street." *Inventing the Melting Pot: The New Immigrants and What it Means to be American*. Edited by Tamar Jacoby. New York: Basic Books, 2004.

Absurdistan. New York: Random House, 2006.

Super Sad True Love Story. New York: Random House, 2010.

"The New Moscow." *Travel + Leisure*. September 15, 2011. http://www.travelandleisure.com/articles/the-new-moscow (accessed July 12, 2015).

"O.K., Glass: Confessions of a Google Glass Explorer." *New Yorker*. August 5, 2013. http://www.newyorker.com/magazine/2013/08/05/o-k-glass (accessed August 2, 2015).

Little Failure. New York: Random House, 2014.

"'Out of My Mouth Comes Unimpeachable Manly Truth': What I Learned from Watching a Week of Russian TV." *New York Times*. February 18, 2015. http://www.nytimes.com/2015/02/22/magazine/out-of-my-mouth-comes-unimpeachable-manly truth.html?_r=0 (accessed July 9, 2015).

"Bellow after Death." *New York Review of Books*. May 10, 2015. http://www.nybooks.com/blogs/nyrblog/2015/may/10/saul-bellows-comedy-death-and-desire/ (accessed June 14, 2015)

Secondary Sources

Al-Shawaf, Rayyan. "Gary Shteyngart's Greatest Muse: Gary Shteyngart." *Globe and Mail*, January 18, 2014, R16.

Anonymous. "Finance and Economics: Stranger than Fiction; China's Currency." *Economist*, January 22, 2011, 85–86.

Antrim, Taylor. "The Coming-of-Age-in-Eastern-Europe Novel." *New York Times Magazine,* December 15, 2002. http://www.nytimes.com/2002/12/15/magazine/the-year-in-ideas-coming-of-age-in-eastern-europe-novel-the.html (accessed April 2, 2015).

Arnett, Peter. "Major Describes Move." *New York Times,* February 8, 1968, 14.

Bakhtin, Mikhail, and Patricia Sollner. "Rabelais and Gogol: The Art of Discourse and the Popular Culture of Laughter." *Mississippi Review* 11.3 (Winter/Spring 1983): 34–50.

Barr, Marleen S. "America and Books Are 'Never Going to Die': Gary Shteyngart's *Super Sad True Love Story* as a New York Jewish 'Ustopia.'" In *Blast, Corrupt, Dismantle, Erase: Contemporary North American Dystopian Literature,* edited by Brett Josef Grubisic, Gisèle M. Baxter, Tara Lee. Waterloo: Wilfrid Laurier University Press, 2014.

Bauman, Zygmunt. *Identity: Conversations with Benedetto Vecchi.* Cambridge: Polity Press, 2004.

Benjamin, Walter. "Moscow." In *Walter Benjamin: Selected Writings.* Part 1, *1927–1930.* Cambridge, Mass.: Harvard University Press, 2005.

Bezmozgis, David. *Natasha and Other Stories.* New York: HarperCollins, 2004.

Blake, David Haven. *Walt Whitman and the Culture of American Celebrity.* New Haven, Conn.: Yale University Press, 2006.

Blumenkranz, Carla. "From Russia with Love Handles: Gary Shteyngart's Less-than-Appetizing Follow-Up." *Village Voice.* May 17–May 23, 2006, 51, 20, C80.

Bojanowska, Edyta M. *Nikolai Gogol: Between Ukrainian and Russian Nationalism.* Cambridge, Mass.: Harvard University Press, 2007.

Boorstin, Daniel J. *The Image: A Guide to Pseudo-Events in America.* New York: Knopf, 2012.

Borenstein, Eliot. "Was It Sexy, or Just Soviet? The Post-Communist Expat Safari Novel Has Its Day." *Nation* 276 (February 3, 2003): 33–36.

Borowitz, Andy. "Mr. Shteyngart's Planet." Review of *Little Failure* by Gary Shteyngart. *New York Times: Sunday Book Review.* January 2, 2014. http://www.nytimes.com/2014/01/05/books/review/little-failure-by-gary-shteyngart.html?_r=0 (accessed June 12, 2015).

Bosman, Julie. "New Novel From Shteyngart Will Be an 'International Thriller.'" *New York Times,* March 25, 2014. http://www.nytimes.com/2014/03/26/business/media/new-novel-from-shteyngart-will-be-an-international-thriller.html?ref=topics (accessed August 2, 2015).

Boyagoda, Randy. "'Little Failure,' by Gary Shteyngart." Review in *Financial Times,* February 14, 2014. http://www.ft.com/cms/s/2/e9b6e876–930a-11e3-b07c-00144feab7de.html (accessed June 14, 2015).

Boym, Svetlana. *Common Places: Mythologies of Everyday Life in Russia.* Cambridge, Mass.: Harvard University Press, 1994.

———. "From the Russian Soul to Post-Communist Nostalgia." *Representations* 49, special issue, "Identifying Histories: Eastern Europe before and after 1989" (Winter 1995): 133–66.

Brown, Sara, and Armando Celayo. "I Am the World, I'll Eat the World." *World Literature Today: A Literary Quarterly of the University of Oklahoma* 83 (March/April 2009): 29–32.

Bulgakov, Sergius. *Unfading Light: Contemplations and Speculations.* Translated by Thomas Allen Smith. Grand Rapids, Mich.: Eerdman's, 2012.

Dickstein, Morris. "Questions of Identity: The New World of the Immigrant Writer." In *The Writer Uprooted: Contemporary Jewish Exile Literature,* edited by Alvin H. Rosenfeld. Bloomington: Indiana University Press, 2008.

Dostoevsky, Fyodor. *The Brothers Karamazov.* Translated by Constance Garnett, adapted by Joseph Cowley. Houston: Strategic Book Publishing, 2015.

Fitzgerald, F. Scott. *The Great Gatsby.* London: Penguin, 2013.

Franco, Dean J. "Globalization's Complaint: Gary Shteyngart's *Absurdistan* and the Culture of Culture." In *Race, Rights, and Recognition: Jewish American Literature Since 1969.* Ithaca, N.Y.: Cornell University Press, 2012.

Franklin, Ruth. "Dechronification." Review of *Super Sad True Love Story* by Gary Shteyngart. *New Republic,* September 2, 2010. http://www.newrepublic.com/article/books-and-arts/magazine/77379/gary-shteyngart-review-dechronification (accessed June 3, 2015).

Friedman, Natalie. "Nostalgia, Nationhood, and the New Immigrant Narrative: Gary Shteyngart's *The Russian Debutante's Handbook* and the Post-Soviet Experience." *Iowa Journal of Cultural Studies* 5 (Fall 2004): 77–87.

Friedman, Robert I. *Red Mafiya: How the Russian Mob Has Invaded America.* New York: Little, Brown, 2009.

Gershenson, Olga, and David Schneer. "Soviet Jewishness and Cultural Studies." *Journal of Jewish Identities* 4 (January 2011): 129–46.

Ghert-Zand, Renee. "Shteyngart's Memoir 'Little Failure' Is Great Success." *Times of Israel,* February 20, 2014. http://www.timesofisrael.com/shteyngarts-memoir-little-failure-is-great-success/ (accessed June 3, 2015).

Giddens, Anthony. *Runaway World: How Globalization Is Reshaping Our Lives.* New York: Routledge, 2003.

Glass, Loren. *Authors Inc.: Literary Celebrity in the Modern United States: 1880–1980.* New York: New York University Press, 2004.

Gogol, Nikolai. *Dead Souls.* Translated by Richard Pevear and Larissa Volokhonsky. New York: Random House, 1996.

Greene, David. *Midnight in Siberia: A Train Journey into the Heart of Russia.* New York: W. W. Norton & Company, 2014.

Grinberg, Marat. "The Hollowing of Gary Shteyngart." *Commentary* 138, no. 1 (July/August 2014): 69–71.

Gwynne, Kate. "10 Authors Who Excel on the Internet." *Guardian,* May 11, 2015. http://www.theguardian.com/books/2015/may/11/10-authors-who-excel-on-the-internet (accessed July 22, 2015).

Hafford, Michael. "Little Failures: Michael Hafford Interviews Gary Shteyngart." *Guernica: A Magazine of Art & Politics,* March 3, 2014. https://www.guernicamag.com/interviews/little-failures/ (accessed June 2, 2015)

Hoashi, Lisa. "Absurdistan." *Missouri Review* 29, no. 3 (2006): 187–88.

Horowitz, David. "I'm a Uniter, Not a Divider." *Salon.com,* May 6, 1999. http://www.salon.com/1999/05/06/bush_2/ (accessed May 28, 2015)

"Immigrants have to be nuts." *Scotsman.* 21 July 2007. http://www.scotsman.com/lifestyle/culture/books/immigrants-have-to-be-nuts-1–909950 (accessed July 25, 2015).

Isaacson, Walter. *Benjamin Franklin: An American Life.* New York: Simon & Schuster, 2004.

Jefferson, Thomas. "First Inaugural." In *Thomas Jefferson: Writings.* New York: Library of America, 1984.

Kakutani, Michiko. "Love Found Amid Ruins of Empire." Review of *Super Sad True Love Story* by Gary Shteyngart. *New York Times,* July 26, 2010. http://www.nytimes.com/2010/07/27/books/27book.html (accessed July 2, 2015).

———. "Welcome to America. Enjoy the Free Napkins and Straws." Review of *Little Failure* by Gary Shteyngart. *New York Times,* January 6, 2014. http://www.nytimes.com/2014/01/07/books/little-failure-a-memoir-by-gary-shteyngart.html?_r=0 (accessed February 3, 2015)

Kaplan, Justin. *Mr. Clemens and Mark Twain.* New York: Simon & Schuster, 2008.

King, Barry. "Stardom, Celebrity and the Para-Confession." *Social Semiotics* 18 (June 2008): 115–32.

Kirkus Review. *The Russian Debutante's Handbook* by Gary Shteyngart. June 1, 2001. https://www.kirkusreviews.com/book-reviews/gary-shteyngart/the-russian-debutantes-handbook/ (accessed February 12, 2015).

Kirmayer, Laurence J., Eugene Raikhel, and Sadeq Rahimi. "Cultures of the Internet: Identity, Community and Mental Health." *Transcultural Psychiatry* 50 (2013): 165–91.

Kirn, Walter. "Russian Unorthodox." Review of *Absurdistan* by Gary Shteyngart. *New York Times,* April 30, 2006, Sunday Book Review. http://www.nytimes.com/2006/04/30/books/review/30kirn.html?pagewanted&_r=0 (accessed May 22, 2015)

Kovačević, Nataša. "Primitive Accumulation and Neanderthal Liberalism: Victor Pelevin, Gary Shteyngart, and Criminal Eastern Europe." In *Narrating Post/Communism: Colonial Discourse and Europe's Borderline Civilization.* New York: Routledge, 2008.

Kramer, Michael P. "Acts of Assimilation: The Invention of Jewish American Literary History."

Jewish Quarterly Review 103 (Fall 2013): 556–79.

Kriebernegg, Ulla. "Ending Aging in the Shteyngart of Eden: Biogerontological Discourse in a *Super Sad True Love Story.*" *Journal of Aging Studies* 27 (January 2013): 61–70.

Kundera, Milan. *The Unbearable Lightness of Being.* New York: Harper, 1984.

Kurzweil, Ray. *The Age of Intelligent Machines.* Cambridge, Mass.: MIT Press, 1990.

Ladegaard, Jakob. "Cowboys and Vampires: Eastern European Encounters in New American Fiction." *Orbis Litterarum* 70, no. 1 (2015): 32–66.

Lambert, Josh. "The True Name of Gary." *JBooks.com: The Online Jewish Book Community.* http://www.jbooks.com/interviews/index/IP_Lambert_Shtenygart.htm (accessed February 3, 2015).

Lappin, Elena. "An American in Prava." Review of *The Russian Debutante's Handbook* by Gary

Shteyngart. *Guardian,* June 14, 2003. http://www.theguardian.com/books/2003/jun/14/featuresreviews.guardianreview24 (accessed May 2, 2015).

Lederer, William J., and Eugene Burdick. *The Ugly American.* New York: W. W. Norton & Company, 1986.

Lee, Steven S. "*Borat,* Multiculturalism, *Mnogonatsional'nost.*" *Slavic Review* 67 (Spring 2008): 19–34.

Lincoln, Abraham. *Abraham Lincoln: His Speeches and Writings,* edited by Roy Prentice Basler. Cleveland, Ohio: Da Capo Press, 2001.

Lindberg, Gary. *The Confidence Man in American Literature.* New York: Oxford University Press, 1982.

López, Alfred J. "'Everybody Else Just Living Their Lives': 9/11, Race and the New Postglobal Literature." *Patterns of Prejudice* 42, no. 4/5 (2008): 509–29.

McClanahan, Annie. "Bad Credit: The Character of Credit Scoring." *Representations* 126, no. 1 (Spring 2014): 31–57.

Malarek, Victor. *The Natashas: Inside the New Global Sex Trade*. New York: Arcade Publishing, 2004.

Marvin, Carolyn. "Your Smart Phones Are Hot Pockets to Us: Context Collapse in a Mobilized Age." *Mobile Media & Communication* 1 (January 2013): 153–59.

Matthews, Owen. "Pasternak's Shadow." *Foreign Policy* 211 (April/May 2015): 84–85.

Melville, Herman. *Moby-Dick or, The Whale*. New York: Penguin 1992.

Mendelsohn, Daniel. "The Cool War." Review of *The Russian Debutante's Handbook,* by Gary Shteyngart. *New York Magazine,* June 10, 2002. http://nymag.com/nymetro/arts/books/reviews/6083/ (accessed April 2, 2015).

Miller, Laura. "Absurdistan." Review of *Absurdistan* by Gary Shteyngart. *Salon.com,* May 1, 2006. http://www.salon.com/2006/05/01/shteyngart_2/ (accessed May 22, 2015).

Minard, Antone. *Jesus in History, Legend, Scripture and Tradition: A World Encyclopedia*. Santa Barbara, Calif.: ABC-CLIO, 2015.

Moran, Joe. *Star Authors: Literary Celebrity in America*. London: Pluto Press, 2000.

Moynahan, Julian. *Vladimir Nabokov.* Pamphlets on American Writers no. 96. Minneapolis: University of Minnesota Press, 1971.

Nabokov, Vladimir. *Lectures on Russian Literature*. New York: Harcourt Brace Jovanovich, 1981.

———. *Nicolai Gogol*. New York: New Directions, 1961.

———. *Lolita*. New York: Knopf, 2010.

Ness, Patrick. "Absurd Person Singular: Patrick Ness Applauds Gary Shteyngart's Satirical Look at a Former Soviet Republic, Absurdistan," Review of *Absurdistan* by Gary Shteyngart. *Guardian,* June 9, 2007. http://www.theguardian.com/books/2007/jun/09/featuresreviews.guardianreview4 (accessed June 1, 2015).

New Yorker. "Gary Shteyngart Describes His Childhood Obsessions with Maps—The New Yorker." YouTube, posted August 31, 2011. https://www.youtube.com/watch?v=fbXJgzXMiQU (accessed August 2, 2015).

Obatnin, Gennady. "Two Hundred Years of *Poshlost*": *Understanding Russianness.* London: Routledge, 2012.

Patterson, Troy. "Three Days of Vodka with Gary Shteyngart: A Boozy Trip Down Memory Lane—and through Russian History—with the Author of *Little Failure.*" *Slate.com.* January 8, 2014. http://www.slate.com/articles/life/drink/2014/01/gary_shteyngart_on_vodka_three_days_of_drinking_with_the_author_of_little.html (accessed July 12, 2015).

Penguin Random House. "A Backpack, a Bear, and Eight Crates of Vodka." http://www.penguinrandomhouse.com/books/228012/a-backpack-a-bear-and-eight-crates-of-vodka-by-lev-golinkin/ (accessed July 5, 2015).

Phelps, William Lyon. *Essays on Russian Novelists.* Hauppauge, N.Y.: Nova Science Publishers, 2004.

Pomerantsev, Peter. *Nothing Is True and Everything Is Possible: The Surreal Heart of New Russia*. New York: Public Affairs, 2014.

Public Affairs. "Nothing Is True and Everything Is Possible." http://www.publicaffairsbooks.com/book/hardcover/nothing-is-true-and-everything-is-possible/9781610394550 (accessed July 11, 2015).

Reddig, Jesper. "The Unbearable Whiteness of Being: Negotiating Hybridity in Post-Soviet Jewish-American Narrative." In *Mobile Narratives: Travel, Migration and*

Transculturation, edited by Eleftheria Arapoglou, Mónika Fodor, and Jopi Nyman. New York: Routledge, 2013.

"Redfellas." *Economist* 342 (March 15, 1997).

Redmond, Sean. "The Star and Celebrity Confessional." *Social Semiotics* 18 (June 2008): 109–14.

Rotella, Mark. "Fiction into Fact: Gary Shteyngart." *Publisher's Weekly,* December 20, 2013. http://www.publishersweekly.com/pw/by-topic/authors/profiles/article/60456-fiction-into-fact-gary-shteyngart.html (accessed July 8, 2015).

Roth, Philip. *Portnoy's Complaint.* New York: Knopf Doubleday Publishing Group, 2011.

Rovner, Adam. "So Easily Assimilated: The New Immigrant Chic." *AJS Review* 30 (November 2006): 313–24.

"The Russian Mafia." *History Channel.* Season 1, episode 3. 2006.

Scott, A. O. "In the Shadow of Stalin's Foot." Review of *The Russian Debutante's Handbook* by Gary Shteyngart. *New York Times,* June 30, 2002. http://www.nytimes.com/2002/06/30/books/in-the-shadow-of-stalin-s-foot.html (accessed April 3, 2015).

Senderovich, Sasha. "'Little Failure' Is Big Success by Ex-Right-Wing Soviet Jew Who Went to Oberlin, Therapy." Review of *Little Failure* by Gary Shteyngart. *Tablet.* January 6, 2014. http://www.tabletmag.com/jewish-arts-and-culture/books/158056/gary-shteyngart-little-failure (accessed March 3, 2015).

Shostak, Debra. "Roth and Gender." In *The Cambridge Companion to Philip Roth,* edited by Timothy Parrish. Cambridge: Cambridge University Press, 2007.

Simon & Schuster Canada. "Russian Tattoo: A Memoir." http://books.simonandschuster.ca/Russian-Tattoo/Elena-Gorokhova/9781451689822 (accessed July 11 2015).

Slezkine, Yuri. *The Jewish Century.* Princeton, N.J.: Princeton University Press, 2011.

Sternheimer, Karen. *Celebrity Culture and the American Dream.* New York: Routledge, 2011.

Tatarsky, Alexandra. "Land of Plenty? The Russian-Jewish-American-post-Soviet-Immigrant-New York Novel." *Calvert Journal,* April 20, 2015. http://calvertjournal.com/articles/show/3967/land-of-plenty-russian-jewish-american-post-soviet-immigrant-novel (accessed July 5, 2015).

Tennyson, Alfred Lord. "Ulysses." In *Alfred, Lord Tennyson,* edited by Michael Baron. London: Orion Publishing, 2012.

Thier, Aaron. "Love and Hardship." *Nation,* November 1, 2010. http://www.thenation.com/article/love-and-hardship-gary-shteyngart (accessed July 2, 2015).

Tocqueville, Alexis de. *Democracy in America,* vols. 1, 2. Translated by Henry Reeves. New York: Bantam, 2004.

Traps, Yevgeniya. "The Year of the Former Soviet Author." *Forward,* December 28, 2014. http://forward.com/culture/211142/the-year-of-the-former-soviet-author/ (accessed July 11, 2015).

Turgenev, Ivan. *Fathers and Sons.* Translated by Richard Freeborn. Oxford: Oxford University Press, 1998.

Twain, Mark. *The Adventures of Huckleberry Finn.* New York: Penguin Books, 1985.

Vapnyar, Lara. *There Are Jews in My House.* New York: Pantheon Books, 2003.

Waldman, Katy. "It's Time to Stop Praising Authors for Being 'Good at the Internet.'" *Slate,* May 22, 2015. http://www.slate.com/blogs/browbeat/2015/05/22/authors_who_are_good_at_the_internet_sorry_those_lists_are_full_of_nonsense.html (accessed July 3, 2015).

Vinokur, Val. "The Russians Came!" *Boston Review: A Political and Literary Forum*. December 15, 2014. http://www.bostonreview.net/books-ideas/val-vinokur-the-russians-came (accessed August 1, 2015).

Wanner, Adrian. *Out of Russia: Fictions of a New Translingual Diaspora*. Evanston, Ill.: Northwestern University Press, 2011.

———. "Russian Jews as American Writers: A New Paradigm for Jewish Multiculturalism?" *MELUS* 37 (Summer 2012): 157–76.

———. "Moving beyond the Russian-American Ghetto: The Fiction of Keith Gessen and Michael Idov." *Russian Review* 73 (April 2014): 281–96.

Weber, Donald. "Permutations of New World Experiences Rejuvenate Jewish-American Literature." *Chronicle of Higher Education* 51 (September 17, 2004): B.8–B10.

Weinberg, Stephen. "A Designer Universe?" Physlink.com. http://www.physlink.com/Education/essay_weinberg.cfm (accessed June 15, 2015)

Whitman, Walt. "Song of Myself." *Walt Whitman: The Complete Poems*. London: Penguin, 1986.

———. "Walt Whitman, a Brooklyn Boy." *Brooklyn Daily Times*, September 29, 1855, 2.

———. "An English and an American Poet." *Walt Whitman: The Contemporary Reviews*, edited by Kenneth M. Price. Cambridge: Cambridge University Press, 1996.

A Window to Paris (originally titled in Russian *Okno v Parizh*). Directed by Yuri Mamin. Sony Pictures Classics, 1993 (released in U.S. 1995).

Wolitzer, Meg. "Gary Shteyngart's 'Little Failure' Is an Unambivalent Success." Review of *Little Failure* by Gary Shteyngart. *NPR Books*. December 27, 2013. http://www.npr.org/2013/12/27/257551858/gary-shteyngarts-little-failure-is-an-unambivalent-success (accessed May 29, 2015)

Wood, Michael. "Never Say Die." Review of *Super Sad True Love Story* by Gary Shteyngart. *New York Times*, August 6, 2010, Sunday Book Review. http://www.nytimes.com/2010/08/08/books/review/Wood-t.html?_r=0 (accessed June 5, 2015)

Yabroff, Jennie. "The Weight of the Past." Review of *Little Failure* by Gary Shteyngart. *Columbia Magazine*, Spring 2014. http://magazine.columbia.edu/reviews/spring-2014/weight-past (accessed June 6, 2015).

Zalewski, Daniel. "From Russia with Tsoris." *New York Times Magazine*. June 2, 2002. http://www.nytimes.com/2002/06/02/magazine/from-russia-with-tsoris.html (accessed February 2, 2014).

INDEX

"Academy of Moors, The," 4
acculturation. *See* assimilation
acting, 15; self-promotion as, 42
African Americans, 15, 22, 46–47 55, 86, 103, 119n49
Aksyonov, Vasily, 18
Ali, Monica, 41
Allen, Woody, 112, 129n35
alterity, 15, 22, 121n83
Ames, Jonathan, 1
anti-Semitism, 33, 34, 53, 54, 90, 91
Antrim, Taylor, 18
äppärät, 62, 63, 65–66, 71–72, 75. *See also* apparatchik
apparatchik, 9, 63, 65, 71
assimilation, cultural, 14–15, 17, 19, 21–22, 33–36 passim, 38, 45, 104
atheism, 52, 99

Babel, Isaac, 41, 78
babushka, 9, 28–33 passim
Bauman, Zygmunt, 44, 56, 59, 89
Beckman, John, 18
beet generation, the, 78. *See also* Russian American literature
Benjamin, Walter, 64
Bezmozgis, David, 11, 13, 14, 19, 78, 114n21
Bible, the, 4, 59; character names from, 20, 23, 58, 59, 59
blurbs, 1, 78, 98–99
Bolshevism, 64, 81. *See also* communism
Borenstein, Eliot, 18
Borowitz, Andy, 79
Boyagoda, Randy, 79, 107
Bulgakov, Mikhail, 18

capitalism, 7–8, 19, 21, 24, 29–30, 32, 33, 37, 39–41, 48, 49, 58, 64–66
Carter, Jimmy, 3, 82
Cervantes, Miguel de, 42
Champion, Edward, 98
Chekhov, Anton, 4, 15, 41, 60
Christianity, 60, 70–71, 80–81
Cleveland (Ohio), 18, 35, 55, 117n80
Columbia University (creative writing program), 6, 15, 57, 106
commercialism, 40, 67
communism, 7, 8, 33. *See also* totalitarianism
con man. *See* confidence man
confessionals, 60, 85, 106, 128n69
confidence man, 26–28, 32
consumerism, 7, 8, 27, 40, 57, 59, 64, 68, 75, 82
criminality. *See* mafia, Russian
cultural mozaic. *See* multiculturalism
cynicism, 7, 39, 41–49 passim, 60, 65, 70; *See also* idealism

Desai, Kiran, 41, 99
Dickstein, Morris, 35
Dostoyevsky, Fyodor, 41, 92
drugs, 4, 9, 10, 18, 42, 117n12
dystopia, 1, 41, 57- 65 passim, 75

East, the (Eastern Europe), 7, 8, 24, 27, 33, 38. *See also* West, the
emigre. *See* immigrant
ethnicity, 3, 4, 12, 33, 41–42 44, 49, 88–89, 101–2; *See also* identity, ethnic
Eurocentrism, 48
exile, 2, 5–6, 13, 20, 23, 27, 39, 89, 114n21

Fitzgerald, F. Scott, 32, 73–75
Foer, Jonathan Safran, 18, 78, 118n33
Franco, Dean J., 39, 55
Franco, James, 1, 15, 57, 77, 96, 107
Franklin, Benjamin, 96–99, 104–108, passim
Franklin, Ruth, 75
Franzen, Jonathan, 18, 77, 96
Friedman, Natalie, 18–19, 22
Friedman, Robert I., 9

Gershenson, Olga, and Schneer, David, 13, 33, 39, 54
Giamatti, Paul, 1, 57
Giddens, Anthony, 7
globalization, 2, 8, 29, 37, 40, 54, 59, 115n35
Gogol, Nikolai, 12, 18, 24–25, 30; ancestor of Shteyngart, 39, 41–42
Golinkin, Lev, 78
Goncharov, Ivan, 41, 43, 119n49
Gorbachev, Mikhail, 10, 102
Gorokhova, Elena, 78
Gothicism, 58, 72, 75, 91, 116n51
Greenberg, Paul, 18
Greene, David, 78
Grinberg, Marat, 14, 90
Gwynne, Kate, 95

Halliburton (corporation), 49, 119n61
Hasidim, 53–54, 90
Hebrew (language), 3, 4, 46, 59, 88, 94
hedonism, 7, 62, 64, 75
Heller, Joseph, 15, 25, 38, 49, 119
Hemon, Aleksandr, 38
hip hop, 15, 46–47, 103, 119n46, 119n49
Holocaust, the, 4, 35, 51, 58, 113; museum of, in *Absurdistan,* 50, 103
Huxley, Aldous, 62

idealism: Western, 15, 28, 48, 50, 54, 56, 74, 116; communist, 7; *See also* cynicism
identity: American, 41, 38; authorial, 5, 13, 78, 102, 104; comic, 41; ethnic, 57, 87, 101, 102, 121n84; formation of, 2, 6, 7, 20, 21, 27, 66, 78, 89, 95, 106, 109, 112n38; politics of, 2, 4, 17, 18, 26, 32, 35, 39, 42, 48, 49, 51, 84–89; Jewish, 12, 13, 33, 37, 39, 59, 102, 114n21; religious, 3, 53, 92; Russian, 13, 14, 37, 43, 101, 118n29; Russian Jewish, 2, 3, 19, 38, 92; Russian Jewish American 3, 13, 38
immigrant chic, 14, 19, 113n43, 114n21
immigrant: experience, 1–2, 11, 14, 88; identity, 18; fiction, 11, 18–19, 22, 42–43, 88 (*see also* immigrant chic)
individualism, 7, 65–67 passim, 124n39
Iossel, Mikhail, 13
Israel, 5, 50, 83, 87, 91

Jefferson, Thomas, 74
Jesus, 51, 59, 71, 90. *See also* Christianity
Jewish diaspora, 12–13, 90
Judaism, 4, 14, 38, 45, 53, 80, 90–91, 120n75

Kakutani, Michiko, 1
kitsch, 25, 31, 64, 70, 74
Kovačević, Nataša, 7, 19, 33
Kriebernegg, Ulla, 61
Kundera, Milan, 63–64, 74
Kurzweil, Ray, 66

Lederer, William J., and Burdick, Eugene, 29
Lee, Chang-rae, 5, 111n17
Lee, Steven S., 39, 48
Lenin, Vladimir Ilyich, 17, 20, 80–81
Leningrad: birthplace and childhood home of Shteyngart, 2, 6–7, 22; revisited 77–78, 81–82, 93, 106
Lermontov, Mikhail, 23, 25, 41, 90
Lincoln, Abraham, 74
Lindberg, Gary, 26–28
Lolita, 25, 68–69, 75–76
Lopez, Alfred J., 41

mafia, Russian, 9–10, 19, 24–30 passim, 39, 79
Malcolm X, 35, 55
Martin, Carolyn, 61
Marx Brothers, 15
Marx, Karl, 5, 88
McClanahan, Annie, 61, 124n39

media: mass, 8; social, 2, 61–71 passim, 95, 124n43; video, 1, 57, 84, 98, 106–7, 124n47
Mendelsohn, Daniel, 18
mob, Russian. *See* mafia, Russian
Moran, Joe, 15, 100
Moscow, 8, 51, 64, 81, 91, 130n44
Moynahan, Julian, 25, 26
multiculturalism, 4, 14, 15, 19, 38–39, 44–56, 59, 80, 104, 111n17

Nabokov, Vladimir, 14, 18, 24, 25, 40, 41, 68, 78, 89, 99, 118n34
narcotics. *See* drugs
neocolonialism, 19
Ness, Patrick, 38
new immigrant chic. *See* immigrant chic
New World, the, 18, 32, 97. *See also* West, the
New York (city), 5, 18, 40, 45, 56, 74, 77, 82, 86, 87, 91, 98–99, 104, 119n49, 122n8. *See also* Queens, New York
Nikon, Patriarch. *See* true believers
nostalgia, 7, 17, 22, 33, 104, 113n43, 115n46, 121n83, 123n15

Oberlin College, 5, 83, 87–89
oligarchs, 9, 37, 39, 49, 79, 89
organized crime. *See* mafia, Russian
Orwell, George, 61

Patterson, Troy, 101
Phillips, Arthur, 18
Pomerantsev, Peter, 39, 79, 130n44
pop culture, 8
poshlust, 99, 100, 128n13. *See also poshlost*
poshlost (vulgarity), 24–33, 36, 40, 43, 62–73 passim, 76, 92, 99, 108. *See also poshlust*
postcolonialism, 46
post-Soviet Russia, 7–10 passim, 30–33, 39–41, 78–79, 103, 115n46
psychoanalysis, 15, 84, 93, 94, 106, 109, 129n35
Pushkin, Alexander, 4, 23, 90, 92
Putin, Vladimir, 20, 108–9

Queens, New York, 3, 45, 82, 87

racism, 14, 22, 34, 87, 90
religion, 3, 4, 22, 39, 52–53, 67, 70–71, 83, 92, 94, 120n75
Republicanism, 5, 83, 87
Roth, Philip, 15–16, 21, 45, 114n23
Rovner, Adam, 14, 19, 35, 104, 112n38, 121n83
Russian American literature, 1, 2, 11–14, 78, 126n2, 126n6

satire, 2, 4, 5, 9, 12, 13, 17, 20, 24, 27, 30, 38–39, 44, 46, 51, 58, 60–61, 66, 80, 101, 103, 109, 124n47; self-satire, 43, 87
schlemiel, 1, 35, 102, 108
science fiction, 58, 72–73
Scott, A.O., 18
self-parody, 11. *See also* self-satire
sexuality, 2, 15–16, 21, 31, 35, 45, 53, 62, 65, 75, 104, 124n47
Shelley, Mary, 72
Soviet Union, 2–3, 7–8, 11–12, 32; Jews in, 13, 14, 33–4
Stuyvesant High School (NYC), 4–5, 87–88

Tatarsky, Alexandra, 11, 78, 119n61
technology, 2, 57, 61–72, 75, 124n43
television, 4, 8–10, 36, 40, 72, 91, 107–8, 128n69, 130n44
Tennyson, Alfred Lord, 36
Challenge, The 4
Thier, Aaron, 60
Tocqueville, Alexis de, 66–67
Tolstoy, Leo, 4, 15, 41, 92
Toole, John Kennedy, 38
totalitarianism, 7, 57, 62–66, 74, 124n47; *See also* communism
Traps, Yevgeniya, 78
true believers, 51
Turgenev, Ivan, 41–44 passim
Twain, Mark, 25, 52, 96, 100–101

Vapnyar, Laura, 11, 13, 14, 19, 114n21
Vizel, Mikhail, 19

Waldman, Katy, 96

Wanner, Adrian, 12, 14, 19, 39, 42, 53, 102–3
warmongering. *See* Halliburton
Weber, Donald, 14
West, the, 7–10 passim, 24, 27–32 passim, 40, 43, 60, 79, 108, 130n44. *See also* East, the
Westerns, 116n51
Whitman, Walt, 96, 104–8
wild East, the, 40, 108
Wolitzer, Meg, 79

Yabroff, Jennie, 7
YouTube, 95, 106; book trailers on, 1, 15, 57, 77. *See also* media, video

Žižek, Slavov, 48